HOPE FOR HEALING
CHURCH WOUNDS

Bless you Minister
Pray as you bless
others. Colossians 3:12

HOPE FOR HEALING CHURCH WOUNDS

Reaching and Restoring Those Who Have Been Genuinely Hurt by the Local Church

By

Michael D. Gray

ELM HILL

A Division of
HarperCollins Christian Publishing

www.elmhillbooks.com

Hope for Healing Church Wounds
Reaching and Restoring Those Who Have
Been Genuinely Hurt by the Local Church

Published in Nashville, Tennessee, by Elm Hill, an imprint of Thomas Nelson. Elm Hill and Thomas Nelson are registered trademarks of HarperCollins Christian Publishing, Inc.

Elm Hill titles may be purchased in bulk for educational, business, fund-raising, or sales promotional use. For information, please e-mail SpecialMarkets@ ThomasNelson.com.

Unless otherwise noted, all Scripture quotations are from The Holy Bible, New King James Version (NKJV), copyright © by Thomas Nelson, 1984. Scripture quotations indicated (AMP) are from The Holy Bible, Amplified Version, Old Testament copyright © by The Zondervan Corporation, 1965, 1987. Scripture quotations indicated (MSG) are from The Message, © by Eugene H. Peterson, used by permission of NavPress, 1993, 1994, 1995, 1996, 2000, 2001, 2002.

Library of Congress Cataloging-in-Publication Data

Library of Congress Control Number: 2018958222

ISBN 978-1-595559579 (Paperback)
ISBN 978-1-595559647 (Hardbound)
ISBN 978-1-595559890 (eBook)

FOREWORD

Recent documentation and statistics reveal that church-inflicted wounds are a growing problem. The purpose of this book is to develop a Christian model that will offer churches practical steps and instructions on how to reach out and restore those members back to church fellowship who have been hurt by the church. Research was conducted through surveys and interviews with four pastors, five church members, and three non-church attenders in El Cajon, California. This research provided specific training for my care team, as well as helpful guidelines that other churches can use to reach and restore wounded church members back to a healthy relationship with God and fellowship with the local church.

DEDICATION

This project is dedicated to my mother, Marion Ruth Gray, who was a strong and steady example in my life, never giving up when the going got tough. She was abused both verbally and physically by her husband, my father, and lived with much pain throughout her married life. Marion could have divorced her husband early on and would not have been violating Scripture in doing so. She would have had the freedom before God to rid herself of all the pain and suffering. However, for the sake of her children she stayed married. She did not want a divorce to have a future influence on her children. I grew up with the memories of my father's abusive and threatening language and actions toward his family. As the oldest child, he sometimes took out his rage on me.

However, my mother held true to her faith in Jesus Christ throughout this suffering, which set a very strong example for my siblings and me. I attribute my growing faith and trust in God to my mother's determination to hold on to God and his promises no matter how difficult life became.

I am forever grateful for my mother's stand in Christ. Her commitment and strength influenced me to be obedient to God's call to the ministry. When ministry was difficult and I experienced "woundedness,"

I remembered the strength of my mother and her determination to not give up on God, no matter what.

I also dedicate this project to my wife, Jeanne Gray, the love of my life. She has been by my side as my partner in life and ministry for over thirty-five years. We have been through some crazy times, as well as some serious times, some heartbreaking times, some joyful times, and some life-changing times. She encouraged me to keep moving forward with my doctoral program and sacrificed to help make it happen. Without her by my side and her help in so many ways I would not be where I am today. There is no one else I would rather have on this journey with me than Jeanne.

In addition to my mother and my wife, I am grateful to my senior pastor, A. B. Vines, Sr. Dr. Vines loved, encouraged, and supported my wife and me back to ministry when we came to San Diego so beaten up by the hurt from our former church. Dr. Vines believed in me and, through his support, gave me many opportunities to use my gifts at New Seasons Church. He was instrumental in my meeting Dr. Adams, the president of Faith Evangelical Seminary, where I was given an opportunity to complete my doctor of ministry program. Without Dr. Vines, I would not be where I am today in serving the Lord.

TABLE OF CONTENTS

LIST OF FIGURES

ABBREVIATIONS

NKJV   New King James Version
            Thomas Nelson, 1984

AMP   Amplified Version
            Zondervan, 1965, 1987

MSG   The Message
            Eugene H. Peterson; NavPress,
            1993, 1994, 1995, 1996, 2000,
            2001, 2002

CHAPTER ONE

O GOD, WHY ME? WHY THIS?

In his *Christianity Today* article "The Church's Walking Wounded," author Tim Stafford was referring to an old friend, a pastor's wife, who in her letter revealed that she had been deeply wounded by the church. After a lifetime of engagement, she dropped out of active involvement as she indicated to Stafford that she needed to learn how to experience Jesus' love instead of guilt and duty. In response, Stafford made this observation concerning the growing dilemma of this problem: "She reminded me of an epidemic I have been uneasily witnessing. Every time I turn around, I meet another person like her, who feels wounded by the church."[1]

According to George Barna, being wounded by church people is a rising epidemic. He stated in the foreword to Stephen Mansfield's book *Healing Your Church Hurt: What to Do When You Still Love God but Have Been Wounded by His People*:

---

1. Tim Stafford, "The Church's Walking Wounded," *Christianity Today*, March 1, 2003, accessed July 10, 2015, http://www.christianitytoday.com/ct/2003/march/9.64.html

Spiritual injury occurs in churches more often than we would like to admit. My research among unchurched adults reveals that nearly four out of every ten unchurched people (37 percent) in the United States avoid church life because of bad experiences in a church or in relation to churched people.[2]

These statistics, according to Barna, have resulted in twenty-five to thirty million adults who have stayed away from Christian churches because of hurtful treatment experienced at the hands of the body of Christ. Barna admitted that he went through several painful times in church ministry. On one occasion, his pastor disagreed with his theology. Instead of the pastor taking the right action to confront him personally, he chose to avoid Barna and made a public statement about how Barna was out of line in his theology. Barna recounted: "He didn't do it by just bad-mouthing me to a few of the faithful: he wrote an entire book on the subject, using me as his unknowing, voiceless foil."[3] Barna approached his pastor on this move and requested that they resolve their differences; however, the pastor's response was harsh and uncaring. He basically told Barna that if he had a problem with his approach, tough luck. Barna was very wounded by the pastor's actions and his unwillingness to handle the situation as brothers in the Lord. This resulted in Barna and his family seeking another church. On another occasion Barna was hurt because the pastor of this church was jealous of his ministry, which was gaining national attention. Barna was in a leadership position, but his pastor falsely accused him in leadership meetings and to other congregational leaders. This kind of treatment was another blow to Barna and his family. Again, his family had no recourse but to the leave the church. There was a third time he was hurt by the church. The church was a predominantly white congregation where Sunday school

---

2.   George Barna, foreword to *Healing Your Church Hurt: What to Do When You Still Love God but Have Been Wounded by His People*, by Stephen Mansfield (Carol Stream, IL: Tyndale House Publishers, 2010), Kindle edition.

3.   Barna, foreword to *Healing Your Church Hurt*.

teachers and students treated his two adopted Hispanic daughters badly. Ridicule and prejudice made it difficult for Barna and his family to stay with this church family. These are just a few examples of the many church ministers and church members who have had to leave a church because of ill-treatment by the church body or the pastor.

We all want the church to be a place where we can go to worship God with freedom. We all want to be encouraged to grow in becoming more like Christ. We all want a place where we find joy in serving others, a place of safety and unconditional love. No one wants to be part of a church that acts like the world, treating people with judgment and condemnation, or lacking concern and love. I recognize that no church is perfect, but as Barna stated, "it can be a shattering reality when your 'church home' becomes a place of rejection and suffering while you are doing your best to be part of the spiritual family."[4]

Different factors contribute to church members being wounded by the church. As has already been stated, church people wound because of judgmental or condemning attitudes. Others confess a serious lack of trust between church members and their leaders. Still others have observed blatant hypocrisy in the lives of the churched. Another factor is the uncivilized treatment some members suffer at the hands of church members.

The recurrence of wounding church members should not be the norm; however, in my research, this sadly happens more frequently than the church wants to admit. This kind of treatment of God's people only grieves the heart of God. Therefore, it is important that the church takes certain measures to put safeguards in place. In doing so the question arises, "How can the church reach and restore fellowship with God and with God's people those who have been legitimately hurt by the church?"

---

4. Stephen Mansfield, *Healing Your Church Hurt: What to Do When You Still Love God but Have Been Wounded by His People* (Carol Stream, IL: Tyndale House Publishers, 2010), Kindle edition.

Statement of the Problem

Today church wounds are a growing problem. Mansfield described the sad results of those who have been wounded by the church.

> The poisoning of souls through church hurt is killing us. The cause of Christ is hindered because the body of Christ is bruised. Most Christians I know either believe they've been wronged by a church or have friends that do."[5]

Mansfield, a pastor of a growing four-thousand-member church for nearly a decade, saw it all come to an end in what he called a "good old-fashioned church fight." This conflict was so intense it resulted in his leaving that ministry. As he recounted his experience, he suffered isolation, suspicion, and humiliation living in what he called "a vise of pain and hostility."[6]

Mansfield is not the only one who has experienced this kind of pain in church ministry. In my pastoral experience, there have been many wounds by both church members and church leaders in the local church and in church organizations. It has taken me several years to heal from these wounds and be restored back to pastoral ministry. I have learned that God never wastes an experience, and my experience of pain from the church has birthed and empowered a heart of compassion and care for those who have been hurt by the church. God has enabled me to spend a considerable number of hours counseling both believers and nonbelievers who have been wounded emotionally and spiritually by church members and church pastors. In my experience, it has been observed that church hurt can so paralyze a member of the body of Christ that he or she does not desire to return to the local church. Some, in fact, are so wounded that they do not trust any pastor or church member again. It

---

5. Mansfield, *Healing*.

6. Mansfield, *Healing*.

may take years of working through their wounds to ever trust another church. Sadly, some of these wounded people slip into the habit of not going to church, and I have seen that some are caught up in another type of religious practice that is not according to the teachings of the Bible.

In the research for this book, being hurt by the church is observed as a serious, ongoing problem that needs to be addressed, with concrete solutions offered. Therefore, it is important that a plan of action be put in place to reach out to those who have been wounded and love them back to the fellowship of the church. God is a God of restoration, and his church must be the place where that restoration and healing takes place. It is my burden that many churches do not have a plan in place. Even my own church, which truly has a heart to heal wounded people, lacks this structure and concrete plan. We cannot leave the wounded behind; the gospel of Jesus Christ demands it.

It is therefore the purpose of this book to offer, through scholarly resources and field research, concrete solutions for reaching and restoring God's people back to church fellowship. The focus of this book is to first address the problem in a local setting of the church where I minister: New Seasons Church in San Diego, California.

I began by first exploring church hurts of some members of this church in El Cajon, California, where I currently serve as the campus pastor. In addition to interviewing some in this congregation, I interviewed some members of other congregations within the greater El Cajon area. Research was also conducted through a survey given to church members, non-church members, and several pastors in my constituency. Though this research has focused upon the greater El Cajon area, it is my intent to broaden my conclusions and recommendations in order to help facilitate healing and restoration well beyond the immediate research target.

Statement of Limitations

The goal of this book is to address legitimate hurts that church members in my area of ministry have experienced. As previously stated, the purpose of this book is to research those who have been hurt by the church in my central location and congregation. It is not the intention of this book to address hurt feelings church members sometimes have because they dislike something that their church is doing. Nor will it address church members leaving their churches because they do not get their way. Hurt feelings do happen among church members and ministers because preferences are not being met, and even though it is important for Christian people to work these things out, the book is not intended to address these hurts that happen among church members. Secondly, this book will not address the physical abuse that some church members experience at the hands of church pastors and leaders. Addressing being wounded because of physical abuse or sexual misconduct and abuse would require an entirely different focus. Through my research, I have discovered that addressing church wounds is a very broad subject. Therefore, it is necessary to narrow the topic to mainly emotional and spiritual wounds that members experience from the church.

Statement of Purpose

The focus of this book is to answer this question: How can the church in the greater El Cajon area of San Diego, California, reach and restore those people who have been genuinely hurt by the local church? As stated above, this book will first address the problem where I minister at New Seasons Church of El Cajon, California. New Seasons of El Cajon is the second campus of the main church located in Spring Valley, California. I have experienced that in nearly five years of pastoring New Seasons of El Cajon, several people have left the church, some because of past wounds—caused by other church leaders—that have never been healed. I sought to reach out to these members; however, restoration did not take place. Others have decided to stay in spite of past problems in the church. These are the members I interviewed.

In addition to New Seasons, I interviewed some members of other congregations who feel that churches within the greater El Cajon area wounded them. Through the results of these interviews, my goal was to provide a training model that my church, New Seasons, can use to help reach out and restore wounded church members back to the fellowship of New Seasons Church.

Importance of Project

The reason this area of study was chosen was not only personal, but for the overall good of the body of Christ. In more than thirty years of pastoral ministry I have seen the agonizing effects on church members and church ministers who have been legitimately wounded by others within the body of Christ. It is disheartening and very sad. Some of my closest friends who were once in pastoral ministry are no longer serving the Lord in that capacity because of being hurt so deeply by the church. In the current pastorate--a work that involved rebuilding a declining church that was preparing to close its doors--I often meet unchurched people who have been hurt or wounded by the church; most want nothing more to do with "the church."

In this research, I discovered that a very large group of those who are leaving the church are young teens, post high school, who have either personally been wounded or they have seen their parents wounded in the church. And because they do not have sufficient development in their biblical worldview, if they enter college, secular and atheistic professors and the general atmosphere of the college overcome them so that they have no interest in church.

David Kinnaman and Gabe Lyons, in their book *unChristian*, documented that many sixteen- to twenty-nine-year-olds have been hurt by the church and thus have lost respect for the church and no longer attend. Their research showed that "many outside of Christianity, especially younger adults, have little trust in the Christian faith, and esteem for the lifestyle of Christ followers is quickly fading among them."[7] Two out of every five of this age group claim to have "a bad impression of present-day Christianity."[8]

These young people do not have argument with what the Bible says about Christ and salvation. Their negative feelings are a result of how they perceive Christians are treating one another. Referred to as "outsiders" these young people say that "Christians possess bark--and bite. Christians may not normally operate in attack mode, but it happens frequently enough that others have learned to watch their step around us."[9]

The authors (Kinnaman and Lyons) used the term "outsiders" to include atheists, agnostics, and those who embrace other faiths, such as Buddhism, Hinduism, Islam, Mormonism, and Judaism. Anyone who is not a born-again Christian is one of these outsiders. There are roughly twenty-four million in this age group in the United States. And of these young people, most who were involved in a church as teenagers "disengage from church life and often from Christianity in some point during early adulthood, creating a deficit of young talent, energy and leadership in many congregations."[10] Kinnaman and Lyons's research showed that one-fifth of all "outsiders" admitted that they have had a bad experience in a church or with a Christian. These bad experiences are mainly due to seeing the church as hypocritical and judgmental.

---

7. David Kinnaman and Gabe Lyons, *unChristian: What a New Generation Really Thinks about Christianity…and Why It Matters* (Ada, MI: Baker Books, 2014), 11.

8. Kinnaman and Lyons, *unChristian*, 24.

9. Kinnaman and Lyons, *unChristian*, 25.

10. Kinnaman and Lyons, *unChristian*, 23.

The authors reported that their research showed that outsiders "consider us hypocritical saying one thing and doing another—and they are skeptical of our morally superior attitudes. They say...Christians think the church is only a place for virtuous and morally pure people."[11] Also, outsiders think that Christians are too quick to judge others. They say, "We are not honest about our attitudes and perspectives about other people. They doubt that we really love people as we say we do."[12] In addition to these factors, Kinnaman and Lyons reported that most "outsiders" have had painful encounters with the Christian faith. They discovered that one-fifth, regardless of age, admitted "they have had a bad experience in a church or with a Christian that gave them a negative image of Jesus Christ. This represents nearly fifty million adult residents of this country—including about nine million younger outsiders who admit they have significant emotional or spiritual baggage from past experiences with so-called Christ followers."[13] Being hurt by Christianity and the church is far too common among these "outsiders." The authors reported that "such hurtful experiences are part of the stories of nearly one out of every two young people who are atheists, agnostics, or of some other faith."[14] This results in the younger generation of adults forming a greater resistance to the Christian faith at a faster rate. These hurtful experiences leave scars that often prevent them from seeing who Jesus really is.

The authors quoted results of an interview they had with a thirty-five-year-old believer about his views of modern-day Christianity. "Christians have become political, judgmental, intolerant, weak, religious, angry, and without balance. Christianity has become a nice Sunday drive. Where is

---

11. Kinnaman and Lyons, *unChristian*, 29.

12. Kinnaman and Lyons, *unChristian*, 30.

13. Kinnaman and Lyons, *unChristian*, 31

14. Kinnaman and Lyons, *unChristian*, 32

the living God, the Holy Spirit, an amazing Jesus, the love, the compassion, the holiness? This type of life, how I yearn for that."[15]

Alethia J. Simmons, in her dissertation titled "Rescuing the Millennials: Four Essential Lessons Learned and Eight Key Principles to Reclaiming This Generation," pointed out that recent trends reveal the decline of church attendance among younger generations. [16] She documented that a study done by the Barna Group revealed that more than 50 percent of millennials who grew up in Christian churches have either left their faith or left the church by the time they are in their early twenties. According to Simmons, Barna also reported, "Millennials were once faithful, yet still love Jesus, but are skeptical and resistant to Christianity. They call themselves 'spiritual but not religious.'"[17] Additionally, "there is an increase from 44 percent to 52 percent among Millennials who are churchless."[18] This shows an alarming 61 percent of today's young people from ages eighteen to twenty-nine, who were once active in church during their teen years, are now spiritually uninvolved in the church in any way. Quoting the Pew Research Center polling, Simmons reported: "this is the highest percentage of religiously unaffiliated Americans reported in U.S. history."[19]

According to a recent study conducted by the Pew Research Center that researched 35,000 American adults:

---

15. Kinnaman and Lyons, *unChristian*, 35.

16. Alethia J. Simmons, "Rescuing the Millennials: Four Essential Lessons Learned and Eight Key Principles to Reclaiming This Generation" (DMin diss., Liberty Theological Seminary, March 2015).

17. Simmons, "Rescuing," 3. The Barna Research Report cited refers to George Barna and David Kinnaman, "Three Spiritual Journeys of Millennials," posted May 9, 2013, accessed November 10, 2014, https://www.barna.com/research/three-spiritual-journeys-of-millennials/

18. Simmons, "Rescuing," 2.

19. Simmons, "Rescuing."

the research shows the Christian percentage of the population dropping precipitously to 70.6%. In 2007, the last time Pew conducted a similar survey, 78.4% of American adults self-identified as Christian…almost every major branch of Christianity in the United States has lost a significant number of members. More than one-third of Millennials now say they are unaffiliated with any faith, up 10 percentage points since 2007.[20]

Both the book *unChristian* and Alethia Simmons's dissertation tell the story that the church needs to do a better job of representing the character of Christ and his gospel to a skeptical and bruised society of young people who have seen more bad in the church than good. It is my contention that the church as a whole, but pastors in particular, should carry the burden of these "lost sheep" who need to be reached and restored to godly fellowship. It is time that, as Christ's church, we reach out to those within our communities with a hand extended to heal and to restore.

It is my hope that this project will assist in working with a team of people from New Seasons Church to provide training and resources that the team can use to mitigate this malady. It is also my desire that this book will benefit other pastors and churches in their effort of reaching hurt church members and restoring them to church fellowship.

Chapter Summaries

Chapter one is the introduction that has given documentation of the ongoing problem of church members experiencing emotional and spiritual wounds at the hands of church members and ministers. The seriousness of this problem results in thousands who used to be active in church but are now no longer attending because of the hurtful treatment they have experienced by the body of Christ. This chapter not only addressed the problem

---

20. Daniel Burke, "Millennials Leaving the Church in Droves, Study Finds," May 14, 2015, accessed January 2, 2017, http://www.cnn.com/2015/05/12/living/pew-religion-study/

but also outlined areas of limitations that are not included in this book. The chapter described the central focus, which answered the question, "How can the church in the greater El Cajon area of San Diego, California, reach and restore people who have been genuinely hurt by the local church?" This book is not only theoretical, but provides a model for training members of my care ministry at New Seasons Church.

Chapter two will give the biblical and theological Scriptures that address being hurt by the church and cite the major "restoration" passages of Scripture in both the Old and New Testaments. The chapter will also include some ministers in church history who were deeply wounded by their colleagues. It will show how these ministers did not allow their hurts to ruin their calling to the gospel ministry, but rather how their wounds strengthened them for greater impact for the expansion of Christ's church.

Chapter three describes the results of my research from published books, articles, theses, and Internet sites. These were resources that were very helpful to me. They helped me not only understand the problem of being wounded in the church, but offered practical solutions and steps for healing and restoration. It is important to this book to include these works with the hope that the resources used will be helpful in the training of my own care team, but I also hope that these resources will be a help and blessing to anyone reading this book. As stated above it is my hope that other churches will utilize this research and build their own ministry plan for restoring wounded church members.

Chapter four will look at the results of questionnaires, interviews, and personal visits I made to church members, non-church attenders, and pastors who have been wounded by the church. The chapter describes the format of a survey I gave to five church members, four local pastors, and three unchurched neighbors. It also includes the results of that survey and what it reveals about why some have not had closure for their own wounds. These results show, through the responses, why those neighbors I interviewed are not attending any church.

Chapter five develops a training model based upon the research results reported in chapter four. The training model is the tool I used to work with a number of people on my care team. It included these objectives:

1. Distinguishing between legitimate hurts and just fabricated excuses.
2. Demonstrating knowledge of what wounded church members go through and what is generally attributed to the cause of those wounds.
3. Demonstrating an understanding of how to reach these wounded members and help restore them back to church fellowship.
4. Demonstrating a good understanding of how to counsel and minister to those who have been wounded in the church through biblical guidance and instruction.

Chapter six will offer specific solutions for reaching and restoring people back to active church life. Based on working with the care team, I provide suggestive helps that other churches can use to reach out and restore wounded church members back to a healthy relationship with God and fellowship with the local church.

Definitions of Terms

El Cajon

A city in California in east San Diego where I reside and minister. Greater El Cajon has sixty evangelical churches of varying denominations and sizes, including one megachurch.

Hurt

Church members who have been legitimately wounded psychologically and spiritually by church members or authoritarian, unfeeling, or ungodly church leaders. Genuine (legitimate) hurt is hereby distinguished from simply having a bad attitude, an unteachable heart, or ungodly or unrealistic expectations.

Heal

Being genuinely hurt by the church causes emotional, psychological, and spiritual wounds that can affect one's relationship with God and other Christians. To heal from these wounds is a process that first begins by not hardening one's heart. Second, it is having a proper response (exhibiting a godly response) to the pain caused by the hurt. Then, it is allowing God to bring passion and purpose through the pain to help others who have also been wounded.

Reach

To make personal contact (to physically and spiritually reconnect) with those in the local community who have been wounded by a church. Although the goal is to reach out with understanding and godly love to church members who have been hurt, it also includes family members, friends, and coworkers of church members.

Restore (to Christian fellowship)

Bringing a wounded church member back to daily fellowship with the Lord and the life of his/her local church. Often those who have been wounded do not want to return to the assembly where the wounding took place. They usually become inactive in church gatherings of any kind, anywhere. For the purpose of this project, restoring to fellowship means to see a separated church member restored to active involvement in the local church.

Local church

The local assembly of believers who profess faith in and allegiance to Jesus Christ and who are committed to meeting together to worship and serve God in the church and in the community where the church is located for the purpose of spreading the gospel of Christ

Care Team

A group of church members of New Seasons Church that serve in the Care Ministry. Their purpose is to reach out to people in the church and the community. This team works with the Congregational Care Pastor to minister to church and community members' physical, emotional, and spiritual needs. This will be the team where the project of reaching and restoring hurt church members will focus. This team will be trained in how to reach out to those who are wounded and help restore them back to church fellowship.

Defining the "Wounded Church"

I recognize that no local church will ever be perfect because it is made up of sinful people. It has been said: "If you find a perfect church, do not join it, because in doing so, it will not be perfect anymore." Every church member has the capacity to wound others in the body of Christ. However, when people come to church they are looking to be treated differently. If that treatment is not different from how they are treated in the world, great disappointment and pain result.

In his article "The Church's Walking Wounded," Tim Stafford related a poignant example. In his conversation with Pastor Mark Labberton of the First Presbyterian Church of Berkeley, California, Pastor Labberton told about one of his elders who went through a very difficult time. This leader and his family experienced several tragedies—a family death, fire, and financial ruin. All these tragedies produced heavy pain, but the elder admitted that what hurt him the most was the treatment from fellow board members when he raised concerns about the direction in which the church was going. "Of all the things that happened to me," he told Pastor Labberton, "this was the most brutal."[21]

I have seen this kind of treatment happen over and over in years of pastoral ministry, and believe that no church is immune to hurting its members. Even though the church is God's people, saved by grace, the church is still made up of sinners, who have issues and sometimes act sinfully toward their brothers and sisters in the faith. Wounding happens; it is sometimes intentional and sometimes unintentional. However, when it does happen, it causes great pain to those church members involved. Therefore, it is important to understand the characteristics of a hurting church.

1. Abused people: They are wounded because of improper sexual advances, misappropriation of funds, or abused by misuse of pastoral authority.
2. Neglected people: Churches are one place people look to for psychological and spiritual care, but sometimes those expectations are unrealistic.
3. Lonely people: Most church members today come from dysfunctional or broken homes where they need the church to offer acceptance, warmth, and genuine love.
4. Guilt-laden people: Many are weighed down with guilt. "Any institution with high ethical ideals will at times place unfair burdens on people or will be perceived as doing so."[22]
5. Over-involved people: Some church members identify themselves with the ministry that they have, rather than who they are in Christ. We are spiritual beings, not spiritual doings. However, "Churches attract idealists...some idealists become

---

21. Stafford, "Walking Wounded." Accessed July 10, 2015.

22. Stafford, "Walking Wounded."

over-involved, over-identifying themselves with their ministries which can lead to burnout."[23]

In quoting psychologist Archibald Hart, Stafford recognized that people are easily wounded because of stress in their life. "Hart thinks an almost Gnostic spirituality is part of the problem--one in which 'people think they can be spiritual without attending to their bodies or their emotions...you don't have a lot of interest in working at emotional maturity, and people are not learning how to be patient and tolerant.'"[24]

Pastor Francis Anfuso, in "Wounded by the Church," documented the results of an online survey given to more than 600 participants from two healthy churches. One of those was his own church, and he reported that 89 percent of his church members said they had experienced church wounds and 59 percent said they had considered not going to church again because of their bad experience. Things like broken trust, deeper vulnerability, and expecting perfection were the main causes of these wounds. "When trust is broken, due to dishonesty or impropriety, the wounding assaults the core of our being."[25] "When someone is promised a genuine representation of God's heart...and significantly less is delivered, that person feels robbed. A violation has taken place."[26] Because of these hurts, people are showing more and more resistance to Christianity in our times. This is clearly an ongoing problem.

Stafford added in "The Church's Walking Wounded": "The Catholic Church's recent scandals offer many examples, but Catholic priests aren't alone. Protestant leaders, too, make improper sexual advances, misuse

23. Stafford, "Walking Wounded."

24. Stafford, "Walking Wounded."

25. Francis Anfuso, "Wounded by the Church," *Relevant Magazine*, May 26, 2010, accessed January 4, 2016, http://www.relevantmagazine.com/god/church/features/21693-wounded-by-the-church

26. Anfuso, "Wounded."

funds, or abuse their authority."[27] Church wounds also occur because members are neglected. When members perceive neglect, right or wrong, and they feel that no one cares, this leads to hurt. "People come to church expecting to have their lives taken seriously, God taken seriously, and they're thrown into this secularized entertainment mode. They are not taken seriously as souls."[28]

In his book *Wounded Workers: Recovering from Heartache in the Workplace and the Church*, Kirk Farnsworth described how church wounds can occur because of the treatment by pastors and church ministers who are not acting in a Christlike manner toward their members. You have, for example, the narcissistic leader who is all about putting himself first. These leaders like to look good. They do not like to be under any accountability and do not like to be challenged. They can do no wrong. This type of leader wants to get to the top and uses people to get there. In his discussion of what he called "Unmasking the Spiritually Abusive Organization," Farnsworth described these kind of leaders:

> these leaders must always come off looking good, regardless of the situation. But in order to do that, sooner or later they have to mistreat people or spiritually abuse them... Obedience and submission are overly emphasized and backed by shaming techniques. You must play by the rules to gain approval, maintain or grow in spiritual stature, and give the church and its leadership a good name.[29]

It has been my experience with a narcissistic leader that it is more about his good name than the church's good name. Also, a narcissistic leader expects his members to be loyal to him, almost to the degree that loyalty to the leader is emphasized and esteemed more than loyalty to

27. Stafford, "Walking Wounded."

28. Stafford, "Walking Wounded."

29. Kirk E. Farnsworth, *Wounded Workers: Recovering from Heartache in the Workplace and the Church* (Mukilteo, WA: WinePress Publishing, 1998), 90.

Christ. They do not actually admit it; however, by the leader's action of discipline, if one disagrees with him, the leader might as well say, "Obey me rather than God." I have experienced that it is hard to break away from this. That kind of leader is always right, and if one would question him, that person is told or made to feel that he or she is out of the will of God. Farnsworth admitted that "punishment can get pretty severe when you are 'exposed' for being disloyal. It may take the form of being told that God will not bless your family or your business. Or you may be made into a public example in order to keep others in line."[30]

I recently met a young Christian woman who, in telling her story, was spiritually abused by a narcissistic leader. This senior pastor told her and other church members that they were not following the will of God if they did not obey him without any question. There was no freedom in Christ to use her gifts or abilities. She was forced to give up her talents and the passions she had for Christ. As a result, she was caught up in fear and doubt. She battled feelings that things were not right in the church but struggled to question the pastor's methods or teaching for fear of the consequences. Her wounds were clearly caused by the ungodly and controlling actions of this pastor and the church leadership. In fact, her entire life was controlled by this pastor. He set down rules of what she could and could not do. For example, having the desire to marry, she was told she had to remain single, which cut off a relationship that she and the associate pastor desired to have. Obedience to this pastor was over and above her obedience to Christ.

Even though this painful church experience happened several years ago, this young woman is still healing from the wounds caused by her treatment. Thankfully, however, she is on the road to recovery. She has not ended up like some Christians I know, who have not come back from their "woundedness." This young lady is now in a good and healthy

---

30. Farnsworth, *Wounded Workers*, 97.

church where her faith is getting stronger and she is learning to celebrate her freedom in Christ. There are times when she has flashbacks of the pain of her experience. However, she is confident that God will use her experience to help others in the body of Christ.

CHAPTER TWO

WHEN GOD STEPS IN

Being wounded by God's people is not just a present-day problem. The Word of God is replete with examples of people who were wounded by those who were claiming to follow God. Yet, while addressing the hurt and pain, these Scriptures also provide answers for healing and restoration. Our God is a God of healing, and in this chapter I will show from several scriptural texts, in both the Old and New Testaments, the answer to that healing and restoration.

Old Testament Restoration Passages

Exodus 14:14: "And Moses said to the people, 'Do not be afraid. Stand still, and see the salvation of the Lord, which he will accomplish for you today… The Lord will fight for you, and you shall hold your peace." The Israelites faced a huge crisis. They faced the raging Red Sea in front of them and the murderous Egyptian army on their heels. It was an impossible situation in any direction that they turned, but God declared and promised himself as their deliverer. He is the God of salvation. This is a reminder that God delivers when we are facing opposition, hurt, or impossible situations. He restores our souls from emotional hurts and wounds. We need to take to heart Moses' words, "The Lord will fight for you, just remain confident and trusting" [paraphrase mine].

Psalm 23:3: "He restores my soul; he leads me in the paths of righteousness for his name's sake." As David's shepherd, the Lord is a restorer. The word *restores* means to turn back to the original state. To be restored to spiritual health. God refreshes the soul, which is the Hebrew word (*nephesh*) for life. Church hurt and church wounds can take the life out of us spiritually. We may be so wounded that we do not want to have anything to do with God, God's people, or his church ever again. However, God is the one who can bring a person back. He refreshes and restores us back to fellowship with himself and his people.

Psalm 30:11: "You have turned for me my mourning into dancing; you have put off my sackcloth and clothed me with gladness." David testified that God restored his joy. We can be confident that God can replace the mourning, sorrow, and pain with an outlook of spiritual health. In God's restoration, he fills our life with joy and gladness. There is a well-known saying in my church: "Earth has no sorrow that Heaven cannot heal."

Psalm 34:17–19: "The righteous cry out, and the LORD hears, and delivers them out of all their troubles. The LORD is near to those who have a broken heart, and saves such as have a contrite spirit. Many are the afflictions of the righteous, but the LORD delivers him out of them all." This Psalm beautifully describes who God is. When his children cry out to him, he responds with his deliverance. The word *deliver* (Hebrew: *Natsal*) is in the Hiphil Perfect, which indicates that the action of God's deliverance is completed. It is a sure promise that the Lord responds to our need in time of trouble, and brings rescue and restoration. In this Psalm, *deliver* means to snatch away, take away, rescue. Even though the pain and memory of the hurt can remain, the Lord promises to rescue us in our hurts. Verse 18 declares another promise: "The Lord is near to those of a broken heart." *Broken heart* has the image of broken in pieces or brought to the breaking point. Not only is God near to those of a broken heart but also he "saves such as have a contrite spirit" (Psalm 34:18b). A *contrite spirit* connotes the idea of being crushed. Being wounded by the church can lead to one's breaking point. I have experienced this kind of pain, entertaining several times the desire to leave the ministry due to feeling as David did. It is a pain that can crush the spirit, leaving one to feel as if he cannot go on. However, in this Psalm David also reminded those who follow God that there will be afflictions, there will be hurts, there will be painful experiences. "Many are the afflictions" (Psalm 34:19a) encompasses all the evil, harm, threats, and trouble for God's people. But the promise of God's restoration is so clear. "The Lord delivers him out of them all" (Psalm 34:19b). Here the word *deliver* (Hebrew: *Natsal*) is in the Hiphil Imperfect, which indicates that God continues to deliver.

Psalm 42:7, 11: "Why are you cast down, O my soul? And why are you disquieted within me? Hope in God; for I shall yet praise him, the help of my countenance and my God." David is in great distress; he is overwhelmed by his enemies. Verse 7 describes his trouble like one wave after another that does not let up. "Deep calls unto deep at the noise of your waterfalls; all your waves and billows have gone over me." He described the pain of his trouble. He suffered physically (*bones*, verse 10) and emotionally (*mourning*, verse 9). Disquieted in verse 11 means to become disturbed, to mourn, even to wail in pain. However, "hope in God" is a declaration that David knew where to turn. He knew that he could go to the Lord with his hurt, therefore declaring his confidence in God. This Psalm expresses the emotions of those who have been hurt by the church. We must put our "hope in God." I have learned in my church wounds that hoping in God means to wait expectantly, wait with gratitude, and wait with praise to God no matter how painful the hurt. Those who have been wounded by the church should not allow that hurt to turn into bitterness toward God. The Lord will restore because He is our helper. He is "the help of my countenance." The word *help* (Hebrew: *yeshu'ot*) is a beautiful phrase that describes that God is salvation, deliverance, and victory.

Psalm 46:1–10 tells us that:

God is our refuge and strength. A very present help in trouble. Therefore, we will not fear. Even though the earth be removed and though the mountains be carried into the midst of the sea; though its waters roar and be troubled, though the mountains shake with its swelling. The LORD of hosts is with us; the God of Jacob is our refuge. Selah. Come, behold the works of the LORD.

This Psalm describes how the Lord comes to the aid of those who are oppressed. He is a very present help in trouble. I like the phrase "present help," as it describes God as a mighty warrior ready to come to the aid of those who are in distress, affliction, and anguish. God is a present help in trouble for "the Lord of hosts is with us and a refuge." The word *refuge* means a secure stronghold; a fortress that cannot be defeated. Therefore, those who are hurt and wounded are invited to press into the Lord and behold his work of restoration.

Psalm 55:22: "Cast your burden on the LORD, and he shall sustain you; he shall never permit the righteous to be moved." David has experienced great pain through the betrayal of a very close friend. The Amplified Bible gives a picturesque description of this betrayal. "He [my companion] has put out his hands against those who were at peace with him; he has broken his covenant [of friendship and loyalty]. The words of his mouth were smoother than butter, but his heart was hostile; his words were softer than oil, yet they were drawn swords" (Psalm 55:20–21, AMP). In this betrayal, David called on God to rescue him from this terrible pain of being betrayed. A. P. Ross, in *The Bible Knowledge Commentary*, further explained:

> David said he could have borne the oppression of *an enemy* or could
> have hidden from *a foe*, but far worse was the fact that he was betrayed
> by a *close friend*. David addressed the traitor (*it is you*), recalling how
> they worshiped the Lord together with the congregation (*throng*).[31]

---

31. A. P. Ross, "Psalms," in *The Bible Knowledge Commentary: An Exposition of the Scriptures: Old Testament*, ed. by John F. Walvoord and Roy B. Zuck (Wheaton, IL: Victor Books, 1985), 835.

"We who had sweet fellowship together, who walked to the house of God in company" (Psalm 55:13–14, AMP). As painful as this was, David clung to the Lord who will never betray, never disappoint, and never give up on him. God will sustain, God will hold secure, and not allow the righteous, his own, to be moved. The word *sustain* (Hebrew: *khool*) means to support and nourish. The word *moved* has the idea of being shaken off its foundation. A betrayal from a close friend is a deep wound, but not beyond God's healing. This Psalm is a reminder that God is a strong tower and his people are secure in his faithful presence.

David recorded God's faithful care over him. This gave him the strength to stand in his pain. Psalm 109:1–3, 30–31:

> Do not keep silent, O God of my praise. For the mouth of the wicked and the mouth of the deceitful have opened against me; they have spoken against me with a lying tongue. They have also surrounded me with words of hatred, and fought against me without a cause. In return for my love they are my accusers, but I give myself to prayer. I will greatly praise the LORD with my mouth; yes, I will praise Him among the multitude. For He shall stand at the right hand of the poor to save him from those who condemn him.

This Psalm expresses the pain and wounds that David received from those who were against him. He used very descriptive language to tell of this affliction. "'For the mouth of the wicked and the deceitful have opened against me.' Their words cut deeply. 'They have fought against me without a cause.' They were deceitful and hateful and rewarded his friendship with false accusations, reciprocating his good will with evil and hatred."[32] However, in his pain, David was determined to call on the Lord. He declared that God's mercy would secure his deliverance. David was confident that God would deliver him and he would shout God's praise to others in testimony to God acting on David's behalf.

---

32. Ross, *Psalms*, 835.

Psalm 147 accompanies Psalm 109. Psalm 147:3: "He heals the brokenhearted. And binds up their wounds." God loves to do a rebuilding in our lives when we have been wounded and hurt. In the context, the Lord promised to build up Jerusalem after his people are exiled. This rebuilding is a picture that God heals and restores the brokenhearted. It is a lesson that those who turn to him in repentance and humility will be healed and restored spiritually.

There are times when church wounds occur because of the wrongdoing of the one who has been wounded. In my experience, it is rarely a one-way street. Church members are wounded not only because of the wrongful treatment by other members but also because of their wrongdoing in the situation.

New Testament Restoration Passages

John 14:27: "Peace I leave with you, my peace I give to you; not as the world gives do I give to you. Let not your heart be troubled, neither let it be afraid." These are wonderful words of strength and help. Jesus promises to give us his peace; the peace of God spoken in Philippians 4:7, when we are troubled. The Lord's peace guards his followers' lives. In our wounds this truth is what we can claim and on which to hold.

Romans 8:28: "And we know that all things work together for good to those who love God, to those who are the called according to his purpose." Even though it is difficult to see the "good" in being wounded by the church, God promises to bring good from it. He is not surprised when we are wounded and hurt, and in his sovereign control he will work good in that pain. Many who have been wounded in the church have testified that God had used their pain to be a ministry to others. It is difficult to understand how someone who has been hurt is feeling unless we have walked through it ourselves. Those who have come through their hurt and are now restored can be the strongest advocates for those who are still out there who need to be loved and restored back to the church.

1 Peter 5:10: "And after you have suffered a little while, the God of all grace, who has called you to his eternal glory in Christ, will himself *restore, confirm, strengthen,* and *establish* you [emphasis mine]." Peter addressed a people who were facing very dark days of persecution. Our church wounds honestly cannot compare. However, Peter did promise that in the trouble, in the hardship, in the wounds and pain, God, who is and has all grace, will restore, confirm, strengthen, and establish his people. *Restore* (Greek: *katartizo*) has the meaning of being made complete. It is used in the mending of nets in Matthew 4:21: "Going on from there, He saw two other brothers, James the son of Zebedee, and John his brother, in the boat with Zebedee their father, mending (*katartizo*) their nets..." It is also used to describe restoring an erring brother in Christ, as in Galatians 6:1: "Brothers, if anyone is caught in any sin, you who are spiritual should restore (*katartizo*) him in a spirit of gentleness..." The next word, *confirm* (Greek: *sterizo*), has the meaning of support and strength. This is the very word that the Lord Jesus used in his exhortation to Peter in Luke 22:32: "But I have prayed for you, that your faith should not fail; and when you have returned to Me, strengthen (*sterizo*) your brethren." The word *establish* (Greek: *themeliosei*) is an important word that means to ground securely. It occurs in Matthew 7:25 when Jesus talks about the house built upon the rock. This house was securely established for it was built on the solid foundation. In using these four powerful words, Apostle Peter sent a message of encouragement. God is more than able to restore his people and make them strong and steadfast. For those who have been hurt by the church this is a truth to stand on. If we look to the Lord when we've been wounded, he will restore and strengthen our faith, as he heals the hurt and pain.

Hebrews 13:6: "So we can confidently say, 'The Lord is my helper; I will not fear; what can man do to me?'" The word *helper* in this case is not the well-known Greek word *paraclete*, which in Scripture often refers to the Holy Spirit as our helper. The writer used a different word to describe the Lord's help. The Greek word *boetheo* comes from *boe*, meaning to cry, and *theo*, to run. The idea is to run upon hearing a cry. It is a beautiful picture of how quickly God responds to our cries. Like a mother who runs to her hurting child, God runs to our aid and assistance.

These Scriptures are just some examples of how being wounded is a result of the sin nature of fallen man. But God, who is the great healer, restorer, sustainer, and refuge, is always ready to come to his people's aid. In addition to these scriptural passages I felt it important to include some examples of those in church history who were wounded, and how they dealt with those hurts.

Examples from Church History

Examples from Church history show that being hurt by the church is nothing new.

In *George Whitefield: The Life and Times of the Great Evangelist of the Eighteenth-Century Revival,* author Arnold A. Dallimore recorded the painful experiences of evangelist George Whitefield, who was one of the gifted men whom God called to lead England in a great revival in the 1700s.

Under the tutelage of John and Charles Wesley, Whitefield had a transforming conversion that led to his call to ministry. As he began to preach, people recognized that God had anointed him in a special way. He drew great crowds and was known to preach to more than eighty thousand people. However, with this great success came strong opposition. Whitefield ministered during a very spiritually dark time for Britain. It was recorded that one in every six houses was a place of drunkenness from gin. Signs around the city read, "Drunk for one penny, dead drunk for two pence, clean straw for nothing."[33] And the church made little difference in the lives of people who were so far from God. As Whitefield called men to Christ he endured the most painful criticisms. These

33. Arnold A. Dallimore, *George Whitefield: The Life and Times of the Great Evangelist of the Eighteenth-Century Revival*, vol. 1 (Westchester, IL: Cornerstone Books, 1970), 23.

criticisms led to violent acts against him. He recorded in his journal, "I was honored with having a few stones, dirt, rotten eggs, and pieces of dead cats thrown at me."[34] His pulpits were smashed. On one occasion he was beaten. On another occasion a man tried to stab him to death. Cattle were driven through his audiences and one time he preached a sermon while someone tried to urinate on him. Famous men of the age attacked him; men such as William Hogarth. Hogarth was a renowned artist who made a mockery of Whitefield in his paintings, and Alexander Pope, a poet, spoke of Whitefield's delivery as the braying of an ass. Whitefield was also wounded by fellow clergy. One of London's most notable clergymen, the Reverend Richard Venn, DD, rector of St. Antholins, published an article that accused Mr. Whitefield of forcing his way to preach when another minister was appointed to the pulpit. In the article, Dr. Venn called Whitefield the "unlicensed intruder." In a published reply to Dr. Venn, Whitefield's friend explained that Mr. Whitefield was misrepresented, proving the falsity of the charges. However, by this time the distorted account spread wide and remained a fixed image of Whitefield in the minds of many. Whitefield's credibility was damaged. This deeply wounded him. However, how did he deal with this great hurt? In his journal he recorded: "Thou shalt answer for me, my Lord and my God. A little while and we shall appear at the judgment seat of Christ. Then shall my innocence be made clear as the light and my dealings as the noonday."[35]

Whitefield faced a lot of opposition and experienced pain. But the deepest wounds came from his longtime friend, evangelist John Wesley. Wesley and Whitefield strongly disagreed on what the Bible teaches about predestination. Believing that God wanted him to preach against predestination, Wesley printed a sermon entitled "Free Grace," which took away many whom Whitefield led to Christ, branding Whitefield as a heretic.

34. Albert Belden, *George Whitefield, The Awakener* (Nashville, TN: Cokesbury Press, 1930), 6.

35. Dallimore., *George Whitefield*, 229.

In *Healing Your Church Hurt*, Mansfield described how Whitefield dealt with this most painful wound:

> There were hours of crying out to God in anguish. There was the weakened health and the tormented mind that the gall of bitterness leaves. Yet, finally, Whitefield rose above his pain to be the man he had long prayed to be. Had he not, it might have been the end of both the revival and his passion for God. He might have begun to nurse a defiling bitterness… He might have fought back but he did none of these things. Instead he forgave his friend, and even gave Wesley the buildings he had constructed to house his thriving ministry.[36]

Even though Whitefield was deeply hurt by his friend, his example of grace and forgiveness should be an example to us all. Mansfield showed the kind of heart Whitefield had toward his friend. "He also refused to allow any movement to grow up in his name but instead urged his followers to become Methodists under Wesley's leadership. His constant refrain was 'Let the name of George Whitefield perish as long as Christ is exalted.'"[37] I wonder how Whitefield's ministry would have turned out had he not shown Wesley the kind of forgiveness and generosity that he did.

George Whitefield was not the only evangelist at the time who had been wounded by church members and ministers. Another evangelist and revivalist was Jonathan Edwards. Author Iain Murray, in his book *Jonathan Edwards: A New Biography*, documented several examples of opposition toward Edwards. A convention of ministers took place in the Massachusetts Bay area. Edwards and other evangelists were present.

Many ministers accused Edwards of preaching heretical teaching that did not square with what they believed. Edwards tried to answer to the accusation but was met with interruptions and rude behavior. Many

---

36. Mansfield, *Healing Your Church Hurt*, Kindle Edition.

37. Mansfield, *Healing Your Church Hurt*, Kindle Edition.

ministers pleaded for Edwards to be heard but their requests were shut down in strong opposition.

At least one hundred thirty ministers in New England stated their reasons for the opposition toward Edwards:

1. They were offended by the "new" type of preaching, which became common in the Awakening preachers.
2. The Awakening preachers confronted the deadness of these ministers who opposed the revival. Edwards's confrontation incensed these ministers and they never forgot the charge.

Most of these clergy, professors at Harvard and Yale, held to Arminianism. Arminian theology taught that conversion to Christ is a matter that can be determined by human will. "Arminianism had encouraged the common opinion of the unregenerate man that it is in his own power to decide upon his salvation."[38] Murray further explained Edwards's position, which resulted in the painful treatment toward him:

> Edwards' conviction was that the New Testament teaches no *one* experience as being the permanent source of the believer's assurance. There is need of the present and continuing work of the Holy Spirit... Further, Edwards insists, from Scripture, that walking in obedience to God and the comfort of the Holy Spirit belong together (Acts 9:31) and therefore, such assurance as is maintained permanently, without any regard or care for holiness of life, is false assurance.[39]

From the biblical Scriptures to church history, being wounded by others in the church is a problem in each generation. Whitefield and Edwards could have allowed their wounds to finish them. Their potential for higher usefulness for God's kingdom could have been lost in strife,

---

38. Murray, *Edwards*, 211–212.

39. Murray, *Edwards*, 265.

bitterness, and unforgiveness. However, history teaches that facing opposition from Christian friends and the church is often the price of God's calling.

In the next chapter I provide present-day documentation that church wounds are an ongoing dilemma in the church. The authors of this documentation tell the story of the hundreds of church members who have been hurt by the church, and the pain in their testimonies. However, the authors do not leave it there, but provide constructive counsel and wisdom for restoration and healing. I found these books and articles to be helpful resources for personal healing, as well as for the New Seasons Church Care Team, in knowing how to employ practical ways of restoring wounded church members back to a healthy church life, and in formulating a ministry plan that New Seasons can use in doing so.

CHAPTER THREE

WHAT VETERANS OF "WOUNDEDNESS" HAVE SAID

This chapter lists resources which include published books, articles, theses, and Internet sites I used in my research. The following is a list of resources.

Published Books

In Dave Burchett's book *Bring 'Em Back Alive*, he challenged the church to be more active in reaching out to members who have been wounded. His conviction came as a result of hundreds who contacted him to tell their stories. Burchett's burden is that few churches are reaching out to those who have left the church because of being injured in some way. He challenged every pastor to "go to a search engine and type in something like 'ex-Christians.' You will be amazed and heartbroken at what you find."[40] What I discovered on one site were the testimonies of many who are so wounded that they are finished with the local church. Kyle Roberts, in his article "Why Every Christian Should Spend an Hour on ExChristian.net," posted this report:

> There are many out there—many who might be silent about their experiences—who are experiencing deep hurt, confusion, dissonance, and even trauma in the church and sometimes at the hands of Christians and pastors they know. While suffering *can* bring about a deeper faith, that's never an excuse for causing it. And more often than not, when the suffering (or trauma) is caused by the church and its leaders, the victims will walk away and find life elsewhere. Who can blame them?[41]

One such testimony referenced by Roberts is titled "Surviving Religious Trauma and Dealing with Anxiety":

> I left Christianity about two years ago, but the effects of leaving the faith have only begun to erupt. Like many people the study of science and my life experiences started to discourage my desire to continue to the affiliate with the faith. I was very involved in my non-denominational church, which really advocated the idea of "Gods will for your life." The church constantly wanted me to take a path I had no desire in exploring. Being in the children's ministry/being in the prayer band. When all I wanted to do was make music and art.
>
> It was very hard dealing with this especially when on many occasions I was told I should give up art. This amongst the idea that my

---

40. Dave Burchett, *Bring 'Em Back Alive* (Colorado Springs, CO: Waterbrook Press, 2004), 91.

41. Kyle Roberts, "Why Every Pastor Should Spend an Hour on ExChristian.Net," *Patheos*, August 17, 2015, accessed August 1, 2016, http://www.patheos.com/blogs/unsystematictheology/2015/08/why-every-pastor-should-spend-an-hour-on-ex-christian-net/

church community didn't really seem authentic and that God's will wasn't really becoming a reality started becoming way too much. I did so much for God and there was no return not even what I thought Gods will was going to be. (Going to a Christian college and becoming a missionary).

When I stopped going to my church I noticed two things, that all the people I thought were my friends were never actually there for me in real life, and when they found out I wasn't going back that I was being shunned even more. This disgusted me, and made me want to be even less part of it.[42]

As a result of reading many testimonies like that of this young man, Burchett, in *Bring 'Em Back Alive*, offered these steps that the church should take to assist in bringing restoration to those who have been hurt by the church.

1. *Create a culture in which seeking and healing the wounded and abandoned is a top priority.* The church should regularly remind its members through all means of communication that every person in the church matters.
2. *Appoint "helper shepherds" in the church.* When a person or family is absent, the "helper shepherd" would be the first to make sure the church attempts to seek the missing member.
3. *Encourage communication with leadership.* Oftentimes pastors and ministers are not aware that church members are struggling. "If ministers had an opportunity to take healing action quickly, perhaps fewer members would be lost."[43]
4. *Provide electronic connections.* Wounded people need to know that people care about them. Burchett suggested that an email

---

42. Roberts, "Why Every Pastor Should."

43. Burchett, *Bring 'Em Back Alive*, 94–95.

ministry to share concerns and hurts could be established in the church.

5. *Be honest about the church.* When speaking with the wounded, don't make promises that the church cannot deliver in the hopes of luring them back to the church.

In his book *When God's People Let You Down: How to Rise Above the Hurts That Often Occur Within the Church,* Jeff VanVonderen discovered that the wounds we receive at the hands of fellow Christians can cause serious damage. He said that leaving wounds unchecked and unhealed affect how we view ourselves and other Christians, and even how we relate to God.

> For some people, the ruin and disappointment of a bad experience with other Christians is so painful that they exit the church for good… Many walk out the back door of the church and never go back—not to any church. [44]

I have seen that those who are wounded by the church face huge hurdles. They live with a deep sense of mistrust toward church people. Because they find it hard to trust church people, they keep a safe distance emotionally. This distance leads to withdrawal. The wounded withdraw from making an effort to build new relationships with other Christians. They live with the terrorizing risk of opening their hearts again to anyone in a church. Not only is this debilitation emotional, but it affects the wounded physically. There is a physical exhaustion at even the very thought of getting involved with Christian people and the church again.

I have seen in my experience with Christians who have been wounded by the church that there are some who spend a good part of their lives believing that no one really cares. "Nobody really knows my needs. I just

---

44. Jeff VanVonderen, *When God's People Let You Down: How to Rise Above the Hurts That Often Occur Within the Church* (Minneapolis, MN: Bethany House Publishers), 1995.

do not fit in anywhere." This is the farthest from the truth; however, those who are wounded have so swallowed these lies that they paralyze them emotionally and spiritually. But there is good news. In my experience, there is no wound so deep that God cannot heal. VanVonderen offered what I find to be an essential process for healing to take place. He witnessed that if a wounded church member takes these kinds of actions, he or she can be on the road to spiritual restoration. VanVonderen called these the Four R's of Recovery.

The first is rest. When one is wounded, rest from church activity is very important. The emotional and spiritual trauma that hurt brings requires an initial period of rest. The fact is God doesn't love us any less when we don't perform. So in this time of rest it is important to take an honest look inside and listen to your emotions. Evaluate, has busyness masked your true feelings, how hurt, how angry, or how depressed you are? Answer with honesty if you're not doing so much, do you feel you have lost God's approval of you?

I have witnessed that some who are wounded in the church add more activity to their schedule, thinking that if they stay busy for God and add more to their plate the pain will start to dissipate. However, in my own experience, rest is absolutely necessary to recovery. When we do not have the energy emotionally or spiritually to keep going, a crash is unavoidable, and inevitably all that we can do is to dwell upon the hurt and pain. I wish that when I was going through my wounds in the church, I had had this counsel from VanVonderen. Just the opposite occurred. My board of deacons expected me to keep going as their pastor and mask the pain. This led to a crash. I am grateful for an older pastor friend who urged me to get away from the church responsibilities and just rest. I was reluctant to do so, however, feeling a sense of guilt that I would be disappointing my congregation. Trying to work through the wound while not taking this rest led to God stepping in and bringing my ministry to a close.

Rest is definitely important but it does not stand alone. There is the step of rehabilitation. What is meant by rehabilitation is do an honest assessment of why the wound happened in the first place. It is all too easy in the pain to beat yourself up by questioning, "What is wrong with me?" or "What is it about me that I always seem to find these unhealthy relationships and keep getting hurt like this?"

Rehabilitation means being honest about not setting boundaries. From his own experience VanVonderen admitted that some of his wounds were the result of not setting good boundaries spiritually and emotionally. Contrary to what one has been taught in the church or how one may think, it is not wrong or unspiritual to prevent certain Christians or the church to barge into our relationship with God and other Christians. In setting proper boundaries, it's important to do a self-examination. These questions may help: "Do you live by these codes: 'Nice is better than honest,' 'Peace at all costs,' 'It's my job to make sure no one else is unhappy'?" VanVonderen said living by these codes results in the kind of behavior that keeps one bound to the other person. "Instead of telling people when you're hurt, angry, disappointed, or that you disagree, you smile and carry the weight of your feelings or opinions alone, and you pretend not to notice someone's inappropriate behavior when in fact you really do notice it."[45] However, it is possible to learn healthy relationship skills. We don't have to allow others to dictate our lives.

Adding to rest and rehabilitation is recovery. Recovery is releasing the hurt. Release means letting go of the things you cannot change. Those who have followed this step have learned that there is so much freedom in being able to say, "I can't control if people are happy with my efforts, but I can control whether I make the effort." "I can't control that people continue to get themselves in messes, but I can control to not continue to bail them out." "I can't control the bad behavior of church leaders who use their authority to control and shame. But I can control that I won't submit to them or be part of that church." In addition to releasing those outside influences, there is the need to release the expectations we put upon ourselves. I lived much of my early ministry with the expectation that I had

---

45. VanVonderen, *When God's People*, 173–174.

to please everyone. As a pastor, I felt it was my job to please everyone and lived with the belief that I could.

However, trying to live up to the expectations of others made me be very cautious in how I pastored God's people. I was very careful to not say anything that would offend them, or step on anyone's toes. When it came to teaching from the Word of God, I was more afraid of what not to say, rather than to tell my people what God wanted them to hear. I realize now that seeking to live up to people's expectations is not the way God wants His servants to do ministry. In doing ministry this way, I was actually doing God's people a disservice. My life verse is 2 Corinthians 5:9: "whether we are here in this body or away from this body our aim is to please him." My goal is to only please the Lord and be faithful to him. In doing so, God's people will be ministered to according to how God leads.

I have also learned that in declaring the Word of God, one is not going to be popular or liked all the time. The truth will sting. My senior pastor prays before every sermon, words like, "Lord, I pray for a spirit of conviction, of challenge, and of change. For when your people are challenged and convicted by your Word, they are changed by the same power of that Word." Being part of New Seasons Church has strengthened me in how I do ministry. Now, when I preach or teach, I am committed to please an audience of One, the Lord Jesus Christ.

Rest, rehabilitation, and release all lead to restoration. That is taking the risk to opening one's heart again. "There comes a time for acceptance—a time when we unhook our losses, even while feeling the pain, and move on."[46] Unhooking those losses and taking risks involves, first of all, to take the risk to have such an active relationship with God that you trust only in him. He is dependable, reliable, trustworthy, and faithful. Don't live depending on other people, especially in the church, to meet your needs. The truth is that no human can completely meet all of our needs. Everyone is flawed except God. Where the trouble occurs is

---

46. VanVonderen, *When God's People*, 180.

when you put all your focus on a church or ministry leader, instead of on the Lord.

God is our only source, and people are resources. I have experienced that people will let us down regardless of how spiritual they are. God is the only one who is completely faithful, therefore it is important to guard our personal relationship with the Lord. To guard against looking to people as sources, it is important to set those personal boundaries. Take to heart this advise: don't allow "the agendas or needs of others" to dictate your life. You are not the need meter. Only God is.

In the risk of opening your heart, there is a step that a lot of people who are wounded find very difficult and resist. It is the step of offering forgiveness. But giving forgiveness is very important for the process of healing wounds. To many forgiveness feels weak. It's giving up control. However, I have learned that giving forgiveness is likened to releasing a debt. We want the person who has wounded us to pay, and to pay big, but instead, forgiving them is like saying, "You are no longer indebted to me." My senior pastor has often said, when speaking on the importance of forgiveness, that we should forgive others as quickly as God has forgiven us. Christians must be the kind of people who show the kind of forgiveness that God has shown us. We have been forgiven a debt we could never pay. Therefore, when we release the debt of those who have wounded us, we release them from a debt that is less than the one we owe to God. With that said, VanVonderen's book cautions that forgiveness does not mean to minimize the offense and the pain caused. There is no excuse for bad treatment of any kind. However, in the act of forgiving, it is a choice to offer the offender the release from their debt.

One of the greatest teachings on forgiveness is found in Matthew 18:34–35, when the Lord Jesus told the parable about the servant who owed a great deal of money. He was greatly forgiven; however, he refused to forgive a small amount that another servant owed him. Jesus ended this parable with a solid warning: "And his master was angry, and delivered him to the torturers until he should repay all that was due to him. So my heavenly Father also will do to you, if each of you, from his heart, does not forgive his brother his trespasses."

I have experienced a lot of pain in my numerous years of ministry. However, I have learned how important it is to live life with that spirit that is always forgiving. It is important to note that Jesus referred to the "heart" in forgiveness. There have been many times when I have heard from Christian people, "I forgive you"—however, these were just words. Their actions showed that there were still feelings of resentment, ill will, and bitterness. I wanted to reciprocate with that kind of attitude; however, regardless of how deep the pain, the Holy Spirit would convict me, "You need to forgive." I do not want to stand before the Lord someday knowing that I held back forgiveness in my heart toward a fellow member of the body of Christ.

The risk to forgive includes the risk to trust. As a pastor, I have heard these words from hurting Christians: "I can't trust him." "I can't trust her." "She has hurt me too many times." Even though these are real feelings, VanVonderen questioned those responses. "There's no doubt that our trust for others is eroded, even obliterated, when we've been hurt. But is it really accurate to say, 'I can't trust'? I don't believe so."[47]

Just as forgiveness is a choice, so is trust. It is a matter of the will to say, "I will take the risk and trust that this person will be trustworthy. And if the person proves to be untrustworthy, then I choose to not trust him or her again." Trust includes asking this important question: "Where, then, do we get the strength to choose to risk again?" Psalm 118:18 gives the answer: "It is better to take refuge in the Lord than to trust in man. It is better to take refuge in the Lord than to trust in princes." Taking refuge in the Lord means, first and foremost, to depend upon God's trustworthiness. We choose to put our hope in his certain ability to supply what we need, because he never changes.

Another helpful book in my research was *Wounded by God's People: Discovering How God's Love Heals Our Hearts*, by Anne Graham Lotz.

---

47. VanVonderen, *When God's People*, 185.

I recommend Lotz's book to anyone who has been hurt by the church. The book was birthed because of a very painful experience that Lotz and her late husband had with one church family. Her husband had served faithfully as the chairman of the board of deacons, chairman of the men's fellowship, and as an adult Sunday school teacher. Disregarding this faithful service, the vote to reinstate him in these leadership positions resulted in six hundred "no's" in the congregation of eight hundred people.

It was clear that the majority of the church body wanted her husband out. Anne and her husband eventually healed from this wound, but in her telling of the story she admitted that the painful memory of it still lingers. The reason for the hurtful treatment was "our impeachable offense was that we believed, lived by, and taught the Bible as the inerrant, inspired, authoritative Word of God. We were innocent casualties caught up in the political power struggles of a denomination that at that time was battling over this very issue."[48] Out of her pain, Lotz learned some valuable lessons. She urged those who have been wounded to not blame God for the sinful behavior of the people who have caused the wounding. Also, she instructed, be honest about the hurt. Do not cover it up, defend it, rationalize it, or excuse it. She said the best way to heal from the wounds is to be open about them. Wounds hurt. They hurt deeply and it takes time to heal. However, because "God causes all things to work together for good to those who love God..." as it says in Romans 8:28, she said, "God can use our hurts to deepen our compassion for others and strengthen our faith."[49] She warned against becoming bitter when others hurt you. "The way you and I handle being rejected and wounded is critical. Our response can lead to healing...or to even more hurt."[50] I have observed that wounded people tend to hurt other people. They lash out toward others in their pain and some even want others to suffer because

---

48. Anne Graham Lotz, *Wounded by God's People: Discovering How God's Love Heals Our Hearts* (Grand Rapids, MI: Zondervan, 2013), Kindle edition.

49. Lotz, *Wounded*, Kindle edition.

50. Lotz, *Wounded*, Kindle edition.

they are suffering. I have witnessed that kind of behavior in some of the church members I have known. Those who leave the church because of the wound like to take others with them or inflict their pain on other church members.

"When we are wounded we need to be very careful about what happens next. Because in the aftermath we are vulnerable to the enemy of our souls who would seek to use us to wound others."[51] Rather than retaliate, said Lotz, it is much better to pray. Our human default in the pain is to want to retaliate, to get even, and even to wish bad things on those who have caused the wounds. However, what brings healing is to take it to the Lord.

I have experienced the powerful reality of this. God can handle our hurts, as no one knows better those hurts than he does. Jesus was ridiculed, falsely accused, slandered, deserted by his friends, betrayed, and ultimately tortured by evil men. No one knows our pain better than Jesus. Rather than retaliate, which only gives ground to the devil, who is after our hearts, it is much better to pray. It is much better to run to God and cling to his loving presence. In my years of ministry, I had hoped to see more of this attitude. However, sadly, I have seen just the opposite. I have seen many run from the pain, run from the problem, run from the church, and ultimately run from God.

In my church, New Seasons, I recently counseled a new member who had a track record of running from church to church. This member was not willing to deal with the past hurts he had experienced. I urged this member that it was now time to stop running. New Seasons could have been a place for his healing; however, he chose once again to leave because he felt that people did not care about him. This was far from the truth, as many deacons also reached out to him. It is uncertain as to whether or not this brother is in fellowship at another church today. He has put himself out of contact with anyone from my church. Throughout my years of ministry, I have witnessed people quit on the church, and my heart

---

51. Lotz, *Wounded*, Kindle edition.

goes out to them. They are MIA (missing in action) from the church and from God. There is no healing in running away. It is much better to run *to* God. I have experienced that when we run to God healing takes place. And only when we release our hurt to God, by forgiving the one who has wounded, can there be real healing. In giving forgiveness Lotz takes it even further. Take action in your forgiveness. Plan to do something special for the person who has caused the wounds. It can be something simple like a phone call, or a birthday card, or giving them a small gift. Even speaking well of them at a social gathering shows that forgiveness has truly taken place in our hearts.

Dave Burchett in *Bring 'Em Back Alive* added some important principles for forgiveness. First of all, "our ability to forgive is rooted in the depth of our gratitude."[52] None of us deserve the forgiveness we have received from the Lord. The Bible is clear that everyone is guilty, in their sin, of offending a holy God, and is deserving of their punishment. The Lord in his mercy, however, has released all of us from a debt that none of us could pay. As difficult as it might be to forgive those in the church who wound us, Ephesians 4:32 is clear, "forgive as the Lord has forgiven you." Christ has extended the same forgiveness toward us that we see in the gospels. Our Lord Jesus showed mercy to a Samaritan woman who had failed in five marriages; he dealt with a dishonest tax collector; his feet were washed by a prostitute; from within his closest circle, his own disciple denied him. In all of these situations Jesus extended forgiveness and restoration. Does he treat us any differently? Christ's forgiveness should fill us with such gratitude that it overflows into an unswerving willingness to forgive others.

Secondly, forgiveness is an act of trusting God for justice. When church people and ministers wounded me I had to learn this principle. The desire of our human nature is "God, get them, and get them good, for what they have done to me." However, we must leave retribution of any kind to the justice of the Lord. Burchett stated, "Forgiving people

---

52. Burchett, *Bring 'Em Back Alive*, 180.

who have wronged you does not mean they are off the hook for any consequences or judgment that may result from their actions. Forgiveness is a personal act of your will that releases the other person from your condemnation."[53] By offering forgiveness to the offender, we are putting our trust in God to see that his justice will be carried out according to his righteous timing.

Burchett continued on to say, "In time, if you entrust your need for justice to God, you will think less and less of the hurt of the offense."[54] I found that if I focused less on retribution to the offender and more on the sovereign and just character of God, the pain of the offense was not the central focus in my life. Even though it is not easy to forget the hurts, we can choose to not focus on them. I have learned that forgiveness does not mean forgetfulness. It means choosing to no longer hold that offense or past offenses against the offender.

Another principle is "forgiveness does not require reunion."[55] This was a real struggle for me in my "woundedness." I had forgiven those who hurt me and my wife; however, it was difficult for me to trust those church members and leaders. It was even difficult to work with them. I have learned that forgiveness is not the same as reconciliation. Two are needed to reconcile. However, when forgiveness is offered you have no control over the other's person's action. "Your offenders may not respond graciously to your forgiveness."[56]

A fourth principle is that "forgiveness is an act of humility, not martyrdom."[57] True humility is offering the forgiveness willingly and moving on. It is not putting on a mournful face, letting others know that you did the right Christian thing. False humility leads to martyrdom. Thomas

---

53. Burchett, *Bring 'Em Back Alive*, 181.

54. Burchett, *Bring 'Em Back Alive*, 182

55. Burchett, *Bring 'Em Back Alive*, 100.

56. Burchett, *Bring 'Em Back Alive*, 182.

57. Burchett, *Bring 'Em Back Alive*, 183.

Merton translated the wise sayings of godly leaders in the fourth century, and these are still applicable today. "One of the elders was asked what was humility, and he said: 'If you forgive a brother who has injured you before he himself asks pardon.'"[58]

We must remember also that "forgiveness is not denial of the hurt."[59]

Forgiveness is letting the one who has wounded you know how much they have hurt or wounded you. However, it does not mean holding the offense against them. Burchett reminded that "pride will often cause us to not give the person who hurt us the 'satisfaction' of knowing we are wounded. That is absurd. Acknowledge the reality of the injury, but make the choice to be healed."[60]

"Let go of the need to know" is another principle.[61] Author David Stoop, in *Forgiving the Unforgiveable*, said, "People choose the path of bitterness when they get caught up in trying to understand the reasons for the offense. They think, if only they could understand why the other person did what he or she did, they could get over it and let go."[62]

In addition to letting go of the need to know, it's important to let go of the need to be right.[63] Forgiveness requires humility. If we strive to be 100 percent right about an issue, we might win the argument but lose the relationship.

Then there is this principle in forgiveness: "Begin to bless those who hurt you and pray for good things in their life."[64] This is probably the most difficult part of forgiveness. In my wounds, I struggled to bless those

---

58. Burchett, *Bring 'Em Back Alive*, 183.

59. Burchett, *Bring 'Em Back Alive*, 184.

60. Burchett, *Bring 'Em Back Alive*, 184.

61. Burchett, *Bring 'Em Back Alive*, 184.

62. David Stoop, *Forgiving the Unforgiveable* (Grand Rapids, MI: Revell, 2003), 75.

63. Burchett, *Bring 'Em Back Alive*, 185.

64. Burchett, *Bring 'Em Back Alive*, 185.

who hurt me so badly. When we are writhing in pain, we do not want to wish blessing on the offender. But our Lord Jesus reminds us in his clear instruction in Luke 6:27–28 that we are to bless those who do harm to us and pray for those who persecute us: "But I say to you who hear: Love your enemies, do good to those who hate you, bless those who curse you, and pray for those who spitefully use you." The last thing we want to do when we are hurt is to pray for the person who has hurt us. But praying for our enemies can change our attitude toward them. Burchett reminded us we all need forgiveness.

> We put on the glasses of gratitude and grace, and we see people who
> hurt us not as the enemy, but as weak, fallible, needy people just like us.
> We look through their outer garments of pride and confusion and see
> the naked truth of their sin. They are people who need forgiveness (just
> like me) they are sinners saved by grace…just like me and you.[65]

From one who has been deeply wounded and has learned to apply these principles of forgiveness and trust in God to her life, Anne Graham Lotz speaks into the soul of the one who has been wounded by the church.

> Dear wounded one, it's time to close the gate behind you. Don't let the
> memories and the mistreatment, the words and the wounds, the jeal-
> ously and the hypocrisy, the deceit and the dishonesty, the cheap talk
> and the inconsistent walk…ruin the promise of blessing and hope for
> the future. Close the gate. Let go of the past so that you can move for-
> ward into all that God has for you. Let go of your resentment…toward
> others who have misrepresented God to you. Let go of your unforgive-
> ness of those who have hurt you… Let go of your offense with God
> because He allowed you to be wounded…[66]

---

65. Burchett, *Bring 'Em Back Alive*, 185–186.

66. Lotz, *Wounded*, Kindle Edition.

Scholarly Articles and Internet Resources

Since forgiveness is so important in the process of healing, I include counsel from Loren Toussaint, Amy Owen, and Alyssa Cheadle, in their article "Forgive to Live: Forgiveness, Health and Longevity." The article reports the results of a survey that was given to 1,500 adults, aged sixty-six and older, over a three-year period. Only actively professing Christians and nonreligious persons were surveyed. The study examined the effects that forgiveness has on a person's mental, emotional, and spiritual health. "Forgiveness has been linked to a number of health outcomes, health conditions, and psychological factors known to be associated with longevity."[67]

Forgiveness is defined as a "freely made choice to give up revenge, resentment, or harsh judgments toward a person who has caused a hurt, and to strive to respond with generosity, compassion, and kindness toward that person. It is a process that involves reducing negative responses and increasing positive responses toward the person who caused the hurt..."[68] The authors pointed out that forgiveness is not condoning the wrong, excusing it, denying it, or minimizing the hurt. It is being honest about the hurt while also being forthright in offering forgiveness to the one who inflicted it. This study showed that those participants who had faith in God and a connection with the church had more willingness to forgive the wrongs done to them, as they understood that God offers unconditional forgiveness. And having belief in an all-forgiving God provided a reduction of stress and anxiety, especially for the elderly who were surveyed. In fact, the authors reported "this data does support the connection between feeling forgiven by God and better mental and physical health, as well as,

---

67. Loren L. Toussaint, Amy D. Owen, and Alysssa Cheadle, "Forgive to Live: Forgiveness, Health and Longevity," *Journal of Behavioral Medicine* 35 (June 2010): 375.

68. Toussaint, Owen, and Cheadle, "Forgive," 375.

optimism and hope."[69] The study also showed the effects of conditional forgiveness, showing that there is more risk of stress, anxiety, and physical and mental health difficulties. "Placing conditions on offering forgiveness to others adds barriers that can translate into extended duration of unforgiveness and/or decreased frequency of forgiveness, both of which may ultimately yield poorer health and greater mortality risk."[70]

In his book *Healing Your Church Hurt: What to Do When You Still Love God but Have Been Wounded by His People*, Stephen Mansfield offered this additional counsel to those who have been wounded in the church. In the process of healing, he said it is important to ask the right questions:

1. Of the things your critics say about you...it is important to look at criticism honestly. "Even those who hate you and mean to hurt you may still be right about what they see in you."[71] Even our enemies can be our friends. They can be helpful in showing the blind spots that we do not see and our friends would not point out.

2. How did you try to medicate your wounded soul? This is a question I would never have thought of asking. But Mansfield's counsel: "you need to write down every way in which your soul has tried to artificially salve its own hurt or meet its own need. And once you've identified those enemies, you need to repent before God, feed on the Word of God...and give people the right to tackle you hard if you seem likely to stray."[72]

3. A third question is, "Were you clinging to anything that contributed to your church hurt?" "Almost every time I deal

---

69. Toussaint, Owen, and Cheadle, "Forgive," 381.

70. Toussaint, Owen, and Cheadle, "Forgive," 383.

71. Mansfield, *Healing Your Church Hurt*, Kindle Edition.

72. Mansfield, *Healing Your Church Hurt*, Kindle Edition.

with people who have been harmed in a church or Christian organization, I can find something they have been clinging to that has kept them from moving on…"[73]

In summary, these resources have broadened my understanding of what a church member goes through when they have been hurt by the church. Each author gives good counsel of what to do in the pain of those hurts. Recognizing that church wounds can be a problem in any church, this next chapter is the documentation of field research I conducted to assess the problem of church members being wounded in my local area. For this research I used a series of questions that I formulated.

_____

73. Mansfield, *Healing Your Church Hurt*, Kindle Edition.

CHAPTER FOUR

WHAT "WOUNDEDNESS" MEANS FOR YOU

The Research Process

This chapter documents the results of a survey to ascertain past
wounds that took place among church members and non-church
members in my local area of El Cajon, California. The survey consisted of
questions about two areas of church-related pain. The first area was desig-
nated to solicit responses to the questions that dealt with various areas of
"woundedness" that those surveyed might have experienced. The second
area was to find out if those surveyed had been restored from those hurts
and were active in their churches. Those surveyed were in three catego-
ries. The first were five church members between the ages of thirty and
fifty who attend my church. The second category included four ministers
between the ages of thirty and fifty who minister in various churches in
the El Cajon and greater San Diego area. Each of these ministers is within

my denomination. The third category I surveyed was three non-churched neighbors between the ages of forty-five and seventy who live in the El Cajon area.

Section one had six survey questions. Section two consisted of three survey questions. The survey was written in multiple choice form. For each question, an area where the participant could make further comments was provided. I used both the qualitative and quantitative methods to gain an understanding of the experiences each participant has had with being wounded by the church and how they could be restored from those wounds. The survey was kept anonymous and confidential. The participants, although known by me, were not asked their names, church affiliations, or any personally identifying information. The survey was given individually to each participant in paper form. To create this survey, I used such online resources as the "General Survey Questionnaire Template,"[74] The "Church Wounds Survey" given to Rock of Roseville Church,[75] and "The Self-Assessment Exercise" by Jack Watts.[76]

The Wounded Church Survey

The following is the survey as written:

Church Members, Church Ministers, and Non-Church Attenders,

Thank you for your willingness to participate in this questionnaire. It is designed to help me understand how to help church members who

74. Question Pro Survey Software 2016, accessed June 2016, www.questionpro. com/surveyquestionnaire.html

75. Francis Anfuso, "Church Wounds Survey," Rock of Roseville Church, Roseville, CA, accessed July 2016, http://surveymonkey.com/results/SM-N367DCPR

76. Jack Watts, "Self-Assessment Exercise," *Recovering from Religious Abuse* (New York, NY: Howard Books Publishing, 2011), Preface.

have been wounded in the church. This questionnaire will take approximately 5 minutes of your time. Your participation in this study is completely voluntary. There are no foreseeable risks associated with this project. However, if you feel uncomfortable answering any questions, you can withdraw from the survey at any point.

Please note: Background information is optional. This, and all your responses, will remain confidential and anonymous.

High School _____ College Graduate _____ Post Graduate Degrees _____
Age Group: 22–40 _____   40–55 _____   55–75 _____
I am: Church Member _____   Church Minister _____
        I do not attend any church _____

Please note: Circle the response that you feel best answers the question based upon your *experience* or *association*. Feel free to comment on any item you wish.

Question 1:   How many churches have you been a member of?
1–2
3–4
More than 4
Comments _____

Question 2:   How long have you been a member of any church?
1 year or less
1–3 years
3–5 years
More than 5 years
Comments _____

Question 3:   What church affiliation(s) have you been a member of? Please check all that apply.
_____ Baptist

_____ Lutheran

_____ Methodist

_____ Pentecostal

_____ Presbyterian

_____ Catholic

_____ Assembly of God

_____ Church of Christ

_____ Independent

_____ Non-Denominational

_____ Other _____

Comments _____

Question 4:   Do you feel you have been wounded in any of the churches you have been part of? Please check what applies.

_____ Yes.   How many? _____

_____ No

Comments _____

Question 5:   If you have been wounded by any church, which of the following wounds occurred? Please select all that apply to your experience.

_____ Judgmental attitudes by church members or minister(s)

_____ Abuse of authority

_____ Power abuse by the minister(s) of the church

_____ Condemning attitudes by church members

_____ Falsely accused by church members

_____ Condescension

_____ Doctrinal divisions

_____ Leader insensitivities

_____ Believer insensitivities

_____ Pride

_____ Promises unfulfilled

_____ Hypocrisy

_____ Church politics
_____ Church splits
_____ Cliques
_____ Financial: misuse of funds
_____ Inappropriate behavior
_____ Immorality
_____ Verbal abuse
_____ Rejection
_____ Neglect to be cared for
_____ Blame casting
_____ Broken trust
_____ Other _____
Comments _____

Question 6:   Did you at any time consider not going to church again because of your experience?

_____ Yes
_____ No

Question 7:   Have you been significantly healed of these wounds?

_____ Yes
_____ Still in the process
_____ No

Question 8:   On a scale of 1–5 (5 being fully healed), what degree of personal healing have you experienced?

_____ Somewhat healed
_____ Mostly healed
_____ Completely healed

Question 9: Has reconciliation between you and the party/parties involved taken place?

_____ Yes

_____ No

The Results of the Wounded Church Survey

Figure 1:   What age group do you fall in?

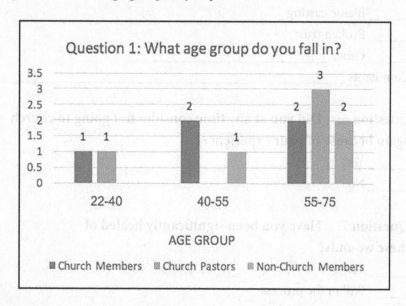

Question 1:   What age group do you fall in? Those who completed the survey were four pastors, ages forty to fifty-five, within my constituency and five members of Christian churches in the El Cajon area, ages forty to sixty. These members are in churches where the congregation ranges from three hundred to six hundred members. The other participants of the survey were non-churched neighbors, ages forty-five to seventy-five.

Figure 2:   How many churches have you been a member of or affiliated with?

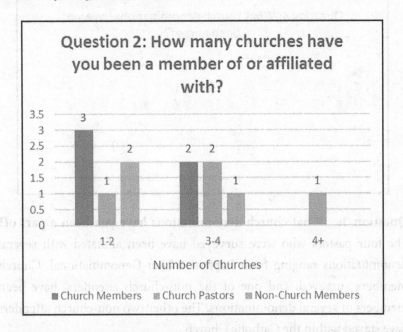

Question 2: How many churches have you been a member of or have been affiliated with? Three of the pastors have been members of four churches, with one pastor holding membership in five churches. Church members who were surveyed have had membership in three to four churches. The non-church attenders have been members of at least two churches. Each participant has been a member of at least one church for five years or less.

Figure 3:   What church denominations have you been a part of?

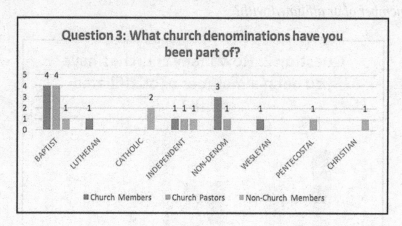

Question 3:   What church denominations have you been a part of?
The four pastors who were surveyed have been affiliated with several denominations ranging from Baptist to Non-Denominational. Church members surveyed, and one of the non-church attenders, have been members of several denominations. The other two non-church attenders have stayed within the Catholic Church.

Figure 4:   Which of the following wounds have you experienced?

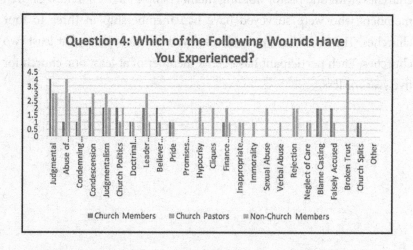

Question 4: **If you have been wounded by any church, which of the following wounds occurred?** The graph reflects those responses. From the four pastors the higher percentages were:

- Judgmental attitudes by church members or ministers (3 out of 4)
- Abuse of authority (all 4)
- Condemning attitudes by church members (2 out of 4)
- Condescension (3 out of 4)
- Being judgmental (3 out of 4)
- Leader insensitivities (3 out of 4)
- Broken trust (4 out of 4)

From the church members the highest percentages were:

- Judgmental attitudes by church members or ministers (4 out of 5)
- Condemning attitudes by church members (2 out of 5)
- Falsely accused by church members (2 out of 5)
- Being judgmental (2 out of 5)
- Blame casting (2 out of 5)

The non-church attenders showed the same response; however, the number was higher, with all three experiencing these areas:

- Judgmental attitudes by church members or ministers (3 out of 3)
- Abuse of authority (3 out of 3)
- Being judgmental (2 out of 3)
- Leader insensitivities (2 out of 3)
- Church politics (2 out of 3)
- Rejection (2 out of 3)
- Neglect to be cared for (2 out of 3)

Figure 5:   Did you at any time consider not going to church again because of the hurts?

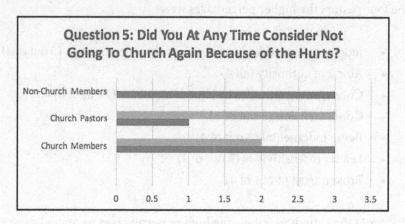

Question 5:   Did you at any time consider not going to any church again because of the hurtful experience? Three out of four pastors responded that their wounds did not affect their quitting on the church. However, among the church members who were surveyed, three out of the five said that they had considered not going back to the church because of their wounds. For the non-church attenders, all three responded with "yes," they had considered quitting on the church.

Question 6:   Have you been significantly healed of the wounds? All four pastors responded "yes." For the church members, four out of five responded "yes," and one member responded, "Still in process." The non-church attenders responded with only one out of the three saying "yes."

Figure 6:   What degree of personal healing have you experienced?

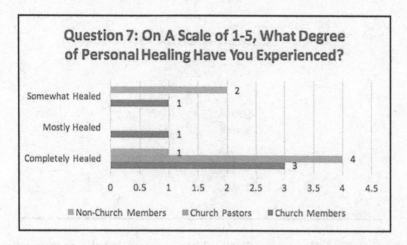

Question 7: On A Scale of 1-5, What Degree of Personal Healing Have You Experienced?

Question 7:   On a scale of 1–5, with 5 being fully healed, what degree of personal healing have you experienced? All four pastors showed a positive response that they have been completely healed of church wounds. However, the church member responses were different. One member said, "Somewhat healed." Another responded that they were "mostly healed." And three members indicated they have been "completely healed." The non-church attenders revealed a different attitude. Only one out of the three said that they have been completely healed of their church hurts.

Figure 7:   Church Members

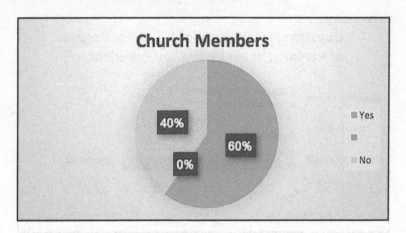

Question 8a: Has reconciliation between you and the party/parties taken place? This graph shows that 60 percent of the church members who were surveyed responded positive. That would indicate that out of the five members who were surveyed, three responded that there has been reconciliation between themselves and those who had wounded them.

Figure 8:   Church Pastors

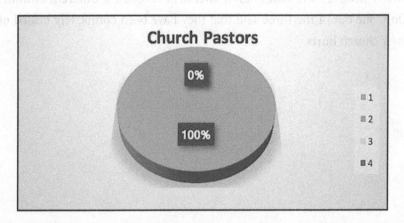

Question 8b: Has reconciliation taken place between you and the party/parties who wounded you? This graph shows that there was a 100 percent response of yes. All four pastors who were surveyed have

experienced reconciliation and healing from the wounds that they have experienced.

In a personal conversation with one of the pastors, I discovered that this pastor's wounds were deep. He was intensely hurt by his former pastor; however, he made an effort to seek out reconciliation. He admitted that had he not done so, he would still be writhing in the pain, and ineffective for leading God's people as a shepherd.

Figure 9:   Non-Church Attenders

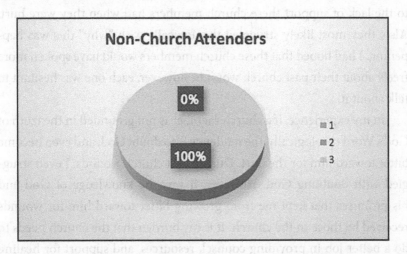

Question 8c: Has reconciliation taken place between you and the party/parties who wounded you? This graph shows that there was a 100 percent negative response for the non-church attenders. This shows that all three non-churchgoers who were surveyed indicated that there has been no reconciliation or resolve to the wounds they experienced in the churches of which they were part.

One of these non-church attenders is a neighbor who I was able to talk with about his and his wife's past hurt in a church. The incident happened more than twenty years ago and so scarred them that they have no interest in church at all. They are now in their seventies.

Response to the Wounded Church Survey

These responses were interesting. All four pastors indicated that reconciliation had taken place with the party or parties who had wounded them. Among the church members, three said that they had received reconciliation; however, for the non-church attenders each one said that no reconciliation had taken place.

I believe these responses indicate that healing among church members had a more difficult journey than for the pastors. This could be due to the lack of support these church members had when they were hurt. Also, they most likely struggled theologically with "why" this was happening. I had hoped that these church members would have spoken more freely about their past church wounds; however, each one was hesitant to talk about it.

In my experience, if a church member is not grounded in the truth of God's Word theologically, the tendency is to doubt God, and even become bitter toward him for the hurt. During past church wounds, I even struggled with doubting God. However, it was the knowledge of God and his promises that kept me from growing bitter toward him for wounds received by those in the church. It is my burden that the church needs to do a better job in providing counsel, resources, and support for healing wounded church members. Based on their responses, I believe that the reason why the non-church neighbors are not involved in any church is because there has been no closure of the wounds they experienced. In my interaction with other non-church attenders in my area of Southern California, many have had a negative, hurtful experience in the church.

From the *Church Wounds* survey in which six hundred church members participated, 89 percent had been wounded in the church. However, 62 percent had been significantly healed of those wounds. The survey revealed that what contributed to this healing was the members' willingness to completely forgive their offenders. And this willingness to forgive came through the healing process occurring within their local church. I believe that this shows how powerful the local church can be for being a place of compassion, grace, and restoration for those who have been wounded. I am grateful that my church, New Seasons, is a place where people find healing. The senior pastor started the church with a heart to reach out and restore people who had been wounded in other churches, as this was his experience. New Seasons is not a perfect church by any means, but it is a place of love, forgiveness, and grace. Part of the mission of New Seasons is to be a spiritual hospital. When I became the pastor of Congregational Care, I learned that the culture of New Seasons is to love and accept everyone. New Seasons has a genuine heart to heal wounded members. However, the structure to do so can be stronger. It is always a challenge to close the back door. Therefore, it is my focus in this book to build a ministry plan that can be used to restore those who have been wounded. In the next chapter I describe this ministry plan and document the results of working with my care team to do so.

CHAPTER FIVE

OFFERING THE HOPE
OF HEALING

Process of Building This Ministry Plan

Over the course of five months I met with members of my church to educate and train them for the purpose of formulating a team designed to reach out to those who have left New Seasons Church because of hurt. I invited ten members from my church; five of these responded. All five members have experienced hurt by other churches with which they have had affiliation. The design of each meeting was to share the information I gained from my research and to discuss and formulate a ministry plan that can be put into place for reaching out to wounded church members. There were a total of five sessions.

In session one, training focused on educating the team on what legitimate church wounds are. I also included what is believed to generally attribute to these wounds and what church members go through when they experience these hurts. It was important for me to make sure that my team had a good understanding of the difference between legitimate wounds and merely fabricated excuses for leaving the church fellowship. In order to do this, I used the resources from chapter three of this book. The team looked at what causes church wounds, such as judgmental and condemning attitudes by church people, the lack of trust between church members and ministers, and uncivilized treatment church members can suffer at the hands of church leaders. Session one included several characteristics of a church that wounds.

Some team members had experienced this kind of behavior in churches with which they had been a part. The characteristics discussed were those such as abusing people, neglect (either intentional or unintentional), church members feeling lonely because no one reached out to them, putting unnecessary guilt on church members, and overtaxing members in service to the church. Recognizing that these things do happen to church members and cause them hurt, I spent a considerable amount of time showing the team that these wounds are nothing new to the church today. Those in biblical times experienced these kinds of wounds. Session one included diligently and extensively going over the Scriptures that I cited in chapter two of this book. Therefore, the training emphasized that any kind of care and restoration administered to those who have been wounded must come from the counsel given by the Word of God. I established with my team that the foundation for a ministry to wounded church members must be God's Holy Word.

Session two covered specific steps for preventing church wounds. This session emphasized that church wounds can be prevented. I stressed that a church needs to become more proactive in safeguarding members from being wounded by the church. As a main resource for understanding what these safeguards are, I referred to Dave Burchett's book *Bring 'Em Back Alive*.

Seeking and Healing the Wounded and Abandoned

The first safeguard is "Create a Culture in Which Seeking and Healing the Wounded and Abandoned Is a Priority."[77] Burchett stressed that the leadership is the most responsible for creating this kind of culture with the church.

The senior pastor of New Seasons often communicates that every person is important, and helping the hurting is a top priority. New Seasons Church is a spiritual hospital. Still, several team members on the care team indicated that New Seasons could do better at this. The church has a large Life Group ministry where members are encouraged to be part of a group. However, with receiving new members each month, there is the challenge of helping these new people assimilate into the life of our church. If members are not connected to a Life Group, it is too easy for those members to feel that they are not being cared for and to slip away. In creating the kind of culture where seeking and healing wounded people become a top priority, this could best be done through the Life Groups, though members would need to be intentional about praying regularly for those who have been wounded and abandoned by the church. In further comment about his idea to create a culture of seeking and reaching out to wounded people, Burchett believes that what is also needed is for churches to establish regular classes or healing seminars for those wounded by the church. He added, "I think that many injured lambs feel alone, and having a forum where they can express the hurt and share their concerns with others would be therapeutic."[78]

This safeguard created some lively discussion with my care team. New Seasons has not had a healing seminar or regular classes on the subject; however, the senior pastor has preached on the importance of reconciliation when people wrong us and we wrong them. Although this is important to teach to the entire church body in sermons, the team

---

77. Dave Burchett, *Bring 'Em Back Alive* (Colorado Springs, CO: Waterbrook Press, 2004), 93.

78. Burchett, *Bring 'Em Back Alive*, 93.

believes that this kind of teaching and training needs to also be filtered through the Life Groups. New Seasons Life Groups are designed to be a member's main support group. Therefore, lessons on healing for those who have been wounded would be important for Life Group members to have so that they can better care for those situations. It is my hope that in addition to this training in the Life Groups, as Burchett suggested, classes on healing will eventually take place as part of the ministry at New Seasons.

Designate and Train Helper Shepherds

Another safeguard is "Designate and Train 'Helper Shepherds' within the Church."[79] The ministry of the "helper shepherds" is to be proactive in noticing when church members are absent and, as a result, to reach out to them.

This is an element of the Deacon Care Ministry, as well as Life Groups, at New Seasons Church. Even with the Life Groups and Deacon Care Ministry there needs to be a separate ministry that focuses on reaching out to members who have been absent. At my church, not every member is part of a Life Group or involved in a ministry of some kind. At services in New Seasons, attendance is not taken, therefore it can be a challenge to check who is absent. However, this is the kind of challenge that I intend to tackle with my care team. It was emphasized in the training that team members will need to be intentional in looking to see which church members are absent or have not been coming to services on a regular basis. It is a standing policy for me, as the campus pastor of New Seasons Church El Cajon, that members who have been absent for more than one Sunday receive a phone call to find out if everything is okay. I consider this kind of concentration to be intentional care for the flock. I believe that every church should have a ministry like this in place. Most of the time a church does well in welcoming new people into the front door, but it has been my experience in other churches where I have served that

---

79. Burchett, *Bring 'Em Back Alive*, 93.

seeking out members who have been absent or not engaged in the church is a weak spot in church ministry. At New Seasons Church the goal is to remind members all the time that their welfare is genuinely cared about, and regularly reaching out to them is one way that New Seasons demonstrates this care.

Encourage Communication with Leadership

A third safeguard recommended by Burchett is to "Encourage Communication with Leadership."[80] Burchett emphasized the importance for the church leadership to be aware of members who struggle with hurt and to make reaching out to them an important practice of the ministry.

At New Seasons this kind of care takes place; however, like anything else, there is always room for improvement. Care for missing members must be intentional and ongoing, as has already been stressed in the previous comments. Even though I make it a priority to reach out weekly to those members who have been absent or disengaged in church life, other members of the church must do the same. Thus, this was an important part in the training. The care team needs to have an "eagle eye" out for those members who are not present in services or other ministries. To make sure that this is happening, care team members will report to the Congregational Care pastor each week the names of those who have not been in church, so that follow-up can take place. The care team members will do this follow-up (see Appendix A).

Offer Electronic Connections

In addition to the third safeguard, Burchett included "Offer Electronic Connections."[81] Have an email ministry where members can share concerns and hurts. Even though this could work, I have discovered that the best way to care for people is face-to-face, or via a phone call. People get

---

80. Burchett, *Bring 'Em Back Alive*, 94.

81. Burchett, *Bring 'Em Back Alive*, 95.

many emails throughout the day and reaching out through an email is a secondary, and a less personal, method to show care.

In discussing this step, care team members felt that there need to be definite safeguards for this kind of email ministry to be effective. People need to feel safe enough to share, and social media and emails can be risky for church members to share their true feelings. It is my experience that most church members do not disclose their true feelings unless they are in a close relationship with the church body. What Burchett suggested to make electronic communication effective is that church members know the church cares about its wounded members. These congregants will more likely communicate their feelings to the church leaders if there is a structure in place, and of course this is only with the wounded member's permission. At present, New Seasons does not have an email system for this kind of forum. The way that I and other ministry leaders discover that a church member is struggling and hurting is through personal contact by that member, or from a close friend of that member who asks permission to share the member's hurts with the New Seasons leadership.

Be Honest About the Church

A fifth safeguard to the training is "Be Honest About the Church."[82] Do not make false promises to church members that the church cannot deliver. I and my team members have seen church members hurt by false promises. One such example is my son who is in pastoral worship ministry. Both the senior pastor and the executive pastor from a church my son attended promised certain things to him and to his wife. During his seven months there, those promises were never fulfilled. The senior pastor told him that he and his family would be cared for, and if there were any struggles that he had with the church, he could go to the senior pastor and the executive pastor and find the security of their support and protection.

In one such meeting, the senior pastor asked my son to share his struggles. My son did so, and the two pastors used this against him and

82. Burchett, *Bring 'Em Back Alive*, 96.

his wife. My son tried to work things out with the senior pastor; however, things grew worse, and these church leaders made it difficult for my son to continue his ministry. It was disheartening for my wife and I to see how this turned out for our son and his family. My son and his wife were both hurt, and had to work through their wounds. In essence, they were "beat up" by the very ones who assured them that they could trust their leadership and authority. As my son and his wife sought another church, they were very cautious. Having gone through similar experiences, my wife and I were able to encourage our son and daughter-in-law during this difficult time.

As a safeguard, the leadership of New Seasons reminds the church body that this is not a perfect church. The senior pastor often says, "We have issues from the pulpit to the back door." In saying this, it is not an excuse to not work hard in taking care of members; however, in the membership classes, members learn that it is a two-way street. People learn up-front the kind of church that New Seasons is. For example, New Seasons Congregational Care Ministry makes it a priority to be there for someone who is hospitalized or in need of physical care because of illness; nonetheless, if the member does not let the staff know that they are in need, it is not the church's fault that the member is not being attended. At New Seasons Church, members are called to accountability in letting someone within the church know of their situation. Members are also instructed not to expect the church to be a finance office, employment center, physical hospital, or to work miracles. This helps our members to not place unrealistic expectations on the church. Still, the church leadership of pastors, elders, deacons, ministers, ministry directors, and daytime staff pledge to love and be there for members as much as is possible.

Be Patient with Hurt Members

I would add that it is important to be patient with hurt members. Those who are wounded in the church face a huge hurdle of doubt. They struggle with a deep feeling that they cannot trust church people.

Therefore, there needs to be an expressed understanding, patience, and love to win them back.

This second session of training opened up an opportunity for some team members to talk about their own past hurts. It also created an atmosphere for them to talk about what lacks they may see in New Seasons Church in the process of caring for hurt church members. Several team members struggled with being overworked during the early years of the church's development. Because the church was smaller at the time, everyone was asked to do a lot. There was the potential for burnout or feeling used. Having gone through this experience, team members wanted to talk about ways to guard against this, especially for new members. New Seasons is highly committed to help members find a place of service to Christ based on their spiritual gifts and abilities. Some members are very zealous to do a lot of things at the church, and this can lead to burnout. Therefore, the leadership of the church is committed to help these members not take on too much. At New Seasons, our senior pastor and the church staff are committed to help church members take care of their families as their first ministry, and beyond that, only to serve in one or two ministries without trying to do too much.

Session three took place over two meetings through Zoom, a computer program that allows one to meet with other people through electronic devices; however, due to technical difficulties, I could only meet with one member during the first Zoom session. While I was not able to go over the full agenda with just one of the team members, I did use the meeting to discuss and answer questions from this member. The topic of discussion was how to give biblical counsel to those who have been wounded in the church. This team member recognizes that he is not a professional counselor, nor are the rest of the team members. However, they each have a good knowledge of the Scriptures that address being wounded, and the principles for God's restoration. Time was spent discussing scriptural passages that have been helpful to my own restoration. I encouraged this team member to use these Scriptures to help others who have been wounded.

The second Zoom meeting was with the entire team. The focus was on steps for recovery. I referred to the book *When God's People Let You Down: How to Rise Above the Hurts That Often Occur Within the Church* by Jeff VanVonderen. I gave the team VanVonderen's "Four R's of Recovery." Team members could identify with the importance of these recovery steps. Several admitted that they needed to implement the first step of rest from all church activity when they were wounded. Out of guilt, some members continued to serve the church, even in their pain. In emphasizing that for rehabilitation to take place, setting boundaries is important, team members recognized that some wounds occur because church members do not set boundaries with one another or their minister.

I have seen members wounded by pastors because they allowed the pastor to dictate how they should live their lives. One of the areas of church wounds noted is the abuse of pastoral authority. Church members allow the pastor to have control over them. Setting boundaries takes discipline, but is a safeguard against being spiritually railroaded. In addition to rest and rehabilitation, the team discussed the importance of releasing the hurt for recovery. It is too easy to hold on to the pain. Some team members admitted that they have done just that. Releasing the hurt means letting go of the things that you cannot change. A visible and active result of this part of the training was seeing how this step of restoration was ministering to some of the team members who were still dealing with past church wounds. The training showed, therefore, that being part of the team helped these members work through their own restoration.

The fourth step, taking the risk to open your heart again and offer forgiveness to the one who has wounded you, hit a nerve with some team members. They all agreed how important forgiving those who have hurt us is to healing from those wounds. Although it is not an easy step, it is necessary, and in obedience to God. There is very definitely healing power experienced when sincere forgiveness is extended to the one or ones who have wounded us. Everyone on the team has seen too many Christians leave the church and have nothing more to do with it because of their unwillingness to forgive, and their unwillingness to take the risk to trust church leadership and church members again.

Having experienced church hurts and going through my own process of healing, I am grateful that my team members wanted to be used by God to minister to those who have been hurt by the church. These members are committed Christians who want to see wounded Christians healed and active in their relationship to God and his people. I feel confident that this will be an effective team for helping lost church members come back into the church fellowship.

Restoring Wounded Church Members Training Model

Based upon the time that I spent with my care team, and the discussions that came out of that training, I and my care team, have included these guidelines as a training model that our church and other churches can use to minister to hurting and absent church members.

1. Educate what legitimate church wounds look like. It is important to understand that people are hurt by these kinds of wounds:
   - Abuse of authority by church ministers
   - Being rejected by other members
   - Blame casting
   - Being treated in a condescending way by church ministers or members
   - Broken trust by church ministers or members
   - Church politics that divide and cause dissension among church members
   - Church leaders insensitive to the needs and concerns of a church member
   - Church leaders or the church makes promises to members that cannot be fulfilled

- Cliques formed by church members where some are not accepted
- Condemning attitudes by church members
- Financial: misuse of funds by church ministers
- Judgmental attitudes by church members or ministers
- Ministers neglect to care for church members

2. Educate regarding what members go through when they are wounded by the church. Being wounded by the church can have these effects:

   - Many people run from the pain, they run from the problem, they run from the church, and ultimately they run from God.
   - Second, it is hard to let go of the past. If a wounded church member does not let go of the past, they cannot move forward into what God has for them.
   - Another effect is that some spend a good part of their lives believing the lies that no one really cares about their hurt; no one knows their needs. They believe the lie that they just do not fit in any church.
   - There is also a deep sense among the wounded that they cannot trust church people. There is a debilitating caution to keep a distance emotionally, which leads to withdrawal. Those who have been wounded withdraw from making an effort to build new relationships with other Christians. Withdrawal becomes a form of protection for them where they reason that if they do not become involved, they will not get hurt again.

Trust is a key issue. Francis Anfuso said, "When trust is broken due to dishonesty or impropriety, the wounding assaults the core of our being."[83] Anfuso continued, "Those who represent God are often given access to

___

83. Francis Anfuso, "Wounded by the Church," *Relevant Magazine*, May 26, 2010, accessed January 4, 2016, http://www.relevantmagazine.com/god/church/features/21693-wounded-by-the-church

the deepest part of a person's being. When a breach or misrepresentation occurs people feel uncovered and unprotected."[84]

To elaborate on the trust issue: "When someone is promised a genuine representation of God's heart…and significantly less is delivered, that person feels robbed. A violation has taken place."[85] The effects of these wounds are leading people to show greater resistance to Christianity.

3. Educate as to where some of the results of being hurt by the church can lead.

- Church hurt can so paralyze a member of the body of Christ that they do not desire to return to the local church.
- Some, in fact, are so wounded that they do not trust any pastor or church member again. It may take years of working through their wounds to trust another church again, if ever.
- Some who have been hurt by the church slip into the habit of not going to church or being caught up in another type of religious practice that is not according to the teachings of the Bible. They become vulnerable to false teachings.
- Being hurt by the church also puts the wounded into a victim mentality. If the person stays there, there is no healing.

In Dave Burchett's article "When You're Hurt by the Church: Letting Go of Victimhood," he said, "In the Christian walk, hurts are inevitable. Feeling like a victim and deciding to stay there is optional."[86] The following is worth noting.

---

84. Anfuso, "Wounded by the Church."

85. Anfuso, "Wounded by the Church."

86. Dave Burchett, "When You're Hurt by the Church: Letting Go of Victimhood," *Christianity Today*, July 2007, accessed February 25, 2017, http://www.christianitytoday.com/pastors/2007/july-online-only/101304a.html

We must also acknowledge the real possibility that sometimes we choose to remain victims when we have the opportunity to move on. It is a waste of our spiritual potential to fixate on how events of the past could have or should have been different. When we are "shot" by people in the church, we tend to focus on the shooter, not the Healer.[87]

It is important to realize that being wounded and broken is part of God's plan for Christian growth. I refer to 2 Corinthians 12:9 (MSG), and to Apostle Paul when he heard the Lord Jesus say to him in his own pain and infirmity: "My grace is enough; it's all you need. My strength comes into its own in your weakness." The point the apostle makes in this Scripture is that God did not want him to focus on his handicap, "my weakness," but on God's strength through his weakness. We must realize that as long as we make excuses, there will not be healing from our wounds. The man in John 5:8, who had been an invalid for thirty-eight years, is a good example. Jesus asked him if he wanted to be well. The man made an excuse that there was no one to put him in the pool. The man had a victim attitude. Jesus was not satisfied with his excuse. He commanded the man, "Rise, take up your bed and walk." That instant, the man found new strength in his legs. He picked up his bedroll and walked away from his "woundedness." The very thing that he relied on, his bed-roll, the one thing that kept him bound from taking action for healing, the Bible says he took this up in a new way. He rolled it up, carried it with him as he walked in the healing Jesus provided. Making excuses as to "why not" or "I cannot" is crippling. There is no wound so deep that God cannot heal. However, this story shows that the action to healing must be our responsibility. Like the man in the story, we have to leave our victim-hood behind.

Burchett emphasized that "The amount of energy invested in choosing bitterness or choosing healing is probably about the same. But the end results are diametrically different. One choice leaves me paralyzed in the

---

87. Burchett, "When You're Hurt."

past. The other choice gives hope for the future."[88] We must realize that if we nurse victimhood instead of treating the wounds, those wounds can become spiritually life-threatening.

The story is told of a visit General Robert E. Lee paid to a woman in a Kentucky home. The general found that the woman was angry and bitter because of what was left of her special tree in the front yard.

> She was upset that Union artillery fire had ruined the shape and beauty of the tree. She wanted General Lee to share her anger. She wanted the great leader to condemn the Yankees and sympathize with her. Lee paused and quietly said, "Cut it down, my dear madam, and forget it." Lee knew that the ravaged tree would only be a constant reminder of her victimhood. He wisely suggested that the reminder be cut out so she could get on with her life. That tree would never be the same, and her bitterness would not change that fact.[89]

If we are wounded, we would do well to heed the words of General Lee. When hurt by the church, the only answer is to cut out the reminder so that we can get on with our lives.

In this training model I include a good article by Joseph Mattera, "15 Traits of Wounded Warriors," which describes common traits that wounded people display in their interaction with others. Mattera said, "It is well-known that those who have been emotionally damaged tend to inflict their hurt and pain on other people."[90] Here are excerpts from Mattera's article.

---

88. Burchett, "When You're Hurt."

89. Joseph Mattera, "15 Traits of Wounded Warriors," *Charisma*, accessed February 25, 2017, http://www.charismanews.com/opinion/the-pulse/48286-15-traits-of-wounded-warriors?showall=&start=1

90. Joseph Mattera, "15 Traits."

1. Hurt people often transfer their inner anger onto their family and close friends. Often those around them become the recipients of harsh tones and fits of rage.

2. Hurt people interpret every word spoken to them through the prism of their pain. Ordinary words are often misinterpreted to mean something negative towards them.

3. Hurt people interpret every action through the prism of their pain. Emotional pain causes them to suspect wrong motives or evil intent behind...people's actions towards them.

4. Hurt people often portray themselves as victims and carry a "victim spirit." Hurt people have a hard time entering into a trusting relationship...often carrying around a suspicious spirit.

5. Hurt people often alienate others and wonder why no one is there for them. They often continually hurt the ones they love.

6. Hurt people have the emotional maturity of the age they received their hurt.

7. Hurt people are often frustrated and depressed because past pain continually spills over into their present consciousness.

8. Hurt people often erupt with inappropriate emotion because particular words, actions or circumstances "touch" and "trigger" past woundedness.

9. Hurt people often occupy themselves with busyness, work, performance and/or accomplishments as a way of compensating for low self-esteem.

10. Hurt people often attempt to medicate themselves with excessive entertainment, drugs, alcohol, pornography, sexual relationships, or hobbies as a way to forget their pain and run from reality.

11. Hurt people have learned to accommodate their private "false self" or "dark side" which causes them to...lack integrity. Often their private life is different from their public life, which causes hypocrisy and compounds feelings of guilt, condemnation and depression.

12. Hurt people are often self-absorbed with their own pain and are unaware that they are hurting other people.

13. Hurt people are susceptible to demonic deception. Saints who lack emotional health and project their pain onto others cause most of the divisions in the church. Satan works in darkness and deception…hurt people often have destructive habit-patterns… Hence, their mind becomes a breeding ground for satanic infiltration and deception.

14. God often purposely surfaces pain so hurt people can face reality. God often allows conflict because He wants the infection to stop spreading and the person to be healed. God often allows conflict so that people would be motivated to dig deeper into their lives to deal with root causes of destructive thought and habit patterns.

15. Hurt people need to forgive to be released and restored to freedom. John 20:23 says that we have to release the sins of others if we are going to be released. This means that if we do not forgive others then the very thing we have become victimized with will become a part of our life.[91]

In addition to these articles, the ministry model will include a good working knowledge of Scriptures that address being hurt and God's answer for restoration.

Old Testament Scriptures

Psalm 23:3: He restores my soul; he leads me in the paths of righteousness for his name's sake.

Psalm 30:11: You have turned for me my mourning into dancing; you have put off my sackcloth and clothed me with gladness.

Psalm 34:17–19: The righteous cry out, and the LORD hears, and

---

91. Mattera, "15 Traits," accessed February 25, 2017.

delivers them out of all their troubles. The LORD is near to those who have a broken heart, and saves such as have a contrite spirit. Many are the afflictions of the righteous, but the LORD delivers him out of them all.

Psalm 42:7, 11: Why are you cast down, O my soul? And why are you disquieted within me? Hope in God; For I shall yet praise Him, the help of my countenance and my God.

Psalm 46:1–10: God is our refuge and strength. A very present help in trouble. Therefore, we will not fear. Even though the earth be removed and though the mountains be carried into the midst of the sea; Though its waters roar and be troubled, Though the mountains shake with its swelling. The LORD of hosts is with us; the God of Jacob is our refuge. Selah. Come, behold the works of the LORD.

Psalm 55:22: Cast your burden on the LORD, and he shall sustain you; he shall never permit the righteous to be moved.

Psalm 147:3: He heals the brokenhearted. And binds up their wounds.

New Testament Scriptures

John 14:27: Peace I leave with you, my peace I give to you; not as the world gives do I give to you. Let not your heart be troubled, neither let it be afraid.

Luke 6:27–28: But I say to you who hear: love your enemies, do good to those who curse you, and pray for those who spitefully use you.

Romans 12:17–19: Repay no one evil for evil. Have regard for the good things in the sight of all men. If it is possible, as much as depends on you, live peaceably with all men…do not avenge yourselves, but rather give place to wrath; for it is written, "Vengeance is mine, I will repay, says the Lord."

Ephesians 4:32: Be kind to one another, tenderhearted, forgiving one another, even as God in Christ forgave you.

1 Peter 5:10: And after you have suffered a little while, the God of

all grace, who has called you to his eternal glory in Christ, will himself restore, confirm, strengthen, and establish you.

Hebrews 13:6: So we can confidently say, "The Lord is my helper; I will not fear; what can man do to me?"

CHAPTER SIX

RECOVERY AND RESTORATION

Solutions Offered for Recovery and Restoration

This chapter offers specific solutions for reaching and restoring people back to active church life. Based on my work with the care team, I provide suggested helps for other churches to use in reaching out and restoring wounded church members back to a healthy relationship with God and fellowship with the local church.

1. Recognize those church members who have been missing from the church fellowship. It is important to be proactive in checking on church members when they have missed two Sundays of church services. Accountability should rest upon the church leaders first in noticing which members are missing; however, church members should also look out for one another.

2. Make an effort to reach out to missing church members through a phone call or personal visit, if possible. Make email the last

resource in making contact, as email is too impersonal for showing care and concern.

3. Let the absent church member know that they have been missed. Ask if there is anything that we can do to help that member come back. At this point, we do not know if that person is missing because of being hurt by someone or some circumstance in the church. In the course of conversation with the member, do some probing to see if the reason why they are staying away is due to one of the common causes that may lead to church wounds.

4. If a member is staying away because of being hurt, and is open to talk about it, do not question the hurt. Empathize with them. Acknowledge their pain. Be there to listen, understand, and show love.

5. Try to meet with the wounded church member. Ask them if they would be open to a personal visit from you. Ask if you can bring another member of the care team with you on your visit.

6. At the meeting assure the hurt member that you care about what they are going through. Encourage them to not give up on the church. Share with them this counsel from Ken Blue in his book *Healing Spiritual Abuse: How to Break Free from Bad Church Experiences*: If you must leave a church you may go through a painful period of anger, depression or even despair. These are normal responses. Take time to take care of yourself. Resist the well-meaning exhortation of friends who tell you to 'snap out of it' in Jesus name. Resist the temptation to stay away from church because of a bad church experience. There actually are more good churches out there than bad ones. Find a church where you can safely tell your story and heal. Never give up on the church. God doesn't.[92]

7. Do not push the wounded member into coming back to the church. As already mentioned, there may be a lot of pain and

92. Ken Blue, *Healing Spiritual Abuse: How to Break Free from Bad Church Experiences*, (Downers Grove, IL: InterVarsity Press, 1993), 135–136.

mistrust. It is important to stand by this wounded member and love him where he is. If possible, build an unconditional friendship with the wounded member.

One lady of my care team is active in church again because of the unconditional love and care from her friend, also a member of New Seasons Church of El Cajon. This lady stood by as a good friend and encouraged her friend to come to New Seasons but did not push and did not give up on her. The care team member has seen her whole family of adult children active in church as a result. Committed friendship and unconditional love won them over.

8. Remind the church member that there is freedom from the hurt and pain of their "woundedness." Help them to guard against being bitter about what they have experienced. "The burdens of bitterness destroy peace, joy, freedom, and life itself. Bitterness cripples, enslaves, and renders us useless for the kingdom of God…but forgiveness opens the way back to spiritual vitality."[93] Help the church member move toward forgiving the one or ones who have wounded them. It is when they can release the hurt to God that healing can take place. "It may be very hard to forgive those who have wronged us, but Jesus' power is with us in the struggle."[94]

In addition to this step, give the wounded church member some articles and books to read on how to heal from the hurt. As already cited in this book, a good list to include would be:

- Jeff VanVonderen, *When God's People Let You Down: How to Rise Above the Hurts That Often Occur Within the Church*
- Ann Graham Lotz, *Wounded by God's People: Discovering How God's Love Heals Our Hearts*
- David Burchett, *Bring 'Em Back Alive: A Healing Plan for*

93. Blue, *Healing Spiritual Abuse*, 137.

94. Blue, *Healing Spiritual Abuse*, 137.

those Wounded by the Church David Burchett, "When You're Hurt by the Church: Letting Go of Victimhood," *Christianity Today*, July 2007

- Francis Anfuso, *Church Wounds*
- Ken Blue, *Healing Spiritual Abuse: How to Break Free from Bad Church Experiences*
- Stephen Mansfield, *Healing Your Church Hurt: What to Do When You Still Love God but Have Been Wounded by His People*

It may be necessary to encourage the wounded member to seek professional Christian counseling to facilitate healing of the wounds. Oftentimes, the process for healing needs to include healthy biblical counseling. Many ministers and church members have been restored to spiritual health as a result of seeking out those trained in helping believers conquer the pain of the past and become spiritually whole again.

I have been through this kind of counseling several times in my "woundedness." God used trained Christian counselors to help me not only understand the hurts that others caused me, but to understand myself better, and why I allowed those hurts. In the process of this counseling, I was able to forgive my offenders and then move past the hurts toward the restoration I needed to continue in the ministry to which God had called me. Francis Anfuso learned, as well, in his own "woundedness" to come to this resolve:

> If I am still bitter or angry about a past hurt, then I will speak of the person in question in more derogatory terms. If I have been released from the choking pain of past hurts, then my recollection will be laced with mercy instead of judgment. As the Bible indicates, "For judgment is without mercy to the one who has shown no mercy. Mercy triumphs over judgment" (James 2:13, NKJV).

I know I am healed when mercy triumphs over judgment; when my thoughts of people focus more on their need than their offense. May my mercy for others be new every morning."[95]

In 1 Peter 1:6–7, the apostle reminds us of the rich benefits of pain and suffering: "In this you greatly rejoice, though now for a little while, if need be, you have been grieved by various trials, that the genuineness of your faith, being much more precious than gold that perishes, though it is tested by fire, may be found to praise, honor and glory at the revelation of Jesus Christ."

Conclusion

In the movie *Hacksaw Ridge*, it tells the true story of Private Desmond Doss who, in one of the bloodiest battles of WWII, heroically faced heavy machine-gun and artillery fire.

While all of the other soldiers retreated because Japanese troops outnumbered them, Private Doss continued throughout the night, carrying wounded soldiers from the kill zone to the edge of the cliff, which was called Hacksaw Ridge. In his article "The True Story of Hacksaw Ridge and Desmond Doss," author Mike Miller recounted:

The fighting took place on the hellish Maeda Escarpment in April 1945. The battlefield, located on top of a sheer 400-foot cliff, was fortified with a deadly network of Japanese machine gun nests and booby traps. The escarpment, nicknamed Hacksaw Ridge for the treacherously steep cliff, was key to winning the battle of Okinawa.[96]

95. Francis Anfuso, *Church Wounds* (Roseville, CA: Rock of Roseville Church, 2010), 254.

96. Mike Miller, "The True Story of Hacksaw Ridge and Desmond Doss: The Medal of Honor Winner Who Never Fired a Shot," accessed March 11, 2017, people.com/movies/the-true-story-of-hacksaw-ridge-and-desmond-doss-the-medal-of-honor-winner-who-never-fired-a-shot/

As Desmond singlehandedly lowered each soldier down to safety, he would pray to God, "Lord, please help me get one more. Lord, help me get one more." By the end of the night and into the early morning, it was reported that Doss rescued an estimated seventy-five men. Like Private Doss, my prayer is "Lord, help me save one more wounded. Help me save one more." The spiritual battlefield is real and the enemy of our souls thrives on creating conflict and warfare among believers in Jesus Christ. Those wounds are not from machine-gun fire, grenades, or booby traps, but they are just as deadly.

My prayer is that the Lord would give my church the courage to not leave the battlefield until the wounded have been lifted down to the safety and healing power of God's restoration. It is my hope and prayer, that as a result of this book, God will use me and others in my church New Seasons, and beyond, to point those who have been deeply hurt, wounded, and so shattered emotionally that they cannot trust another church or church leader, to the amazing power of God's presence and power for rebuilding their lives emotionally and spiritually. The ache of my wounds was intense and difficult, but I am thankful for those painful experiences that God allowed and even brought into my life, so that I am able to help others know and embrace the fullness of a fresh start and new season in their lives.

The pain of being wounded makes us stronger. It gives us the strength to live with this resolve that no matter what ill-treatment may come, we will continue to believe in God's promises that he is a restorer. We will continue to forgive, even when it is most difficult to do so. And we will trust in the Lord that he does cause all things to work together for his good of conforming each one of his children to the character of Jesus Christ.

APPENDIX A

Report Form to Contact Church Members

Who Have Been Missing for
Two Consecutive Sundays

1. Sunday Date: _____
   Service time (check one):
   New Seasons El Cajon 8:00 a.m. service _____
   New Seasons Spring Valley
   9:00 a.m. service _____   11:00 a.m. service _____

2. Member's Contact Information
   Name: _____
   Phone number: _____
   Email address: _____
   Residence address: _____

3. Care team call to the missing member:

Date: _____

Time: _____

Care team member: _____

Results of the call: _____

_____

_____

Important: Please turn in form to congregational pastor by the following Sunday.

BIBLIOGRAPHY

Anfuso, Francis. "Wounded by the Church." *Relevant Magazine*,
    May 26, 2010. http://www.relevantmagazine.com/god/church/
    features/21693-wounded-by-the-church

Anfuso, Francis and David Loveless. *Church Wounds*. Roseville, CA:
    Rock of Roseville Church, 2010.

Anderson, Neil T. *The Bondage Breaker*. Eugene, OR: Harvest House,
    1990.

Arterburn, Stephen and Jack Felton. *Toxic Faith: Experiencing
    Healing From Painful Spiritual Abuse*. Colorado Springs, CO:
    Waterbrook Press, 2001.

Barna, George and David Kinnaman. *Churchless: Understanding
    Today's Church and How to Connect With Them*. Carol Stream,
    IL: Tyndale House, 2014.

Belden, Albert. *George Whitefield, The Awakener: A Modern Study of
    the Evangelical Revival*. Nashville, TN: Cokesbury Press, 1930.

Blue, Ken. *Healing Spiritual Abuse: How to Break Free From Bad
    Church Experiences*. Downers Grove, IL: IVP, 1993.

Blue, Ken and John White. *Healing the Wounded: The Costly Love of
    Church Discipline*. Westmont, IL: InterVarsity Press, 1985.

Bulkey, Ed. *Only God Can Heal the Wounded Heart*. Eugene, OR: Harvest House Publishers, 1995.

Burchett, Dave. *Bring 'Em Back Alive: A Healing Plan for Those Wounded by the Church*. Colorado Springs, CO: Waterbrook Press, 2004.

Burchett, Dave. "When You're Hurt by the Church: Letting Go of Victimhood." *Christianity Today*, July 2007. http://www.christianitytoday.com/pastors/2007/july-online-only/101304a.html

Burke, Daniel. "Millennials Leaving the Church in Droves, Study Finds," May 14, 2015. http://www.cnn.com/2015/05/12/living/pew-religion-study/

Dallimore, Arnold A. *The Life and Times of the Great Evangelist of the Eighteenth-Century Revival*. Vol. 1. Westchester, IL: Cornerstone Books, 1970.

Enroth, Ronald. *Churches That Abuse*. Grand Rapids: Zondervan Publishing House, 1992.

Farnsworth, Kirk E. *Wounded Workers: Recovering from Heartache in the Workplace and the Church*. Mukilteo, WA: WinePress Publishers, 1998.

Hendricks, William D. *Exit Interviews: Revealing Stories of Why People Are Leaving the Church*. Chicago: Moody Press, 1993.

Jackson, Chris. *Loving God When You Don't Love the Church: Opening the Door to Healing*. Grand Rapids, MI: Chosen Books, 2007.

Johnson, David and Jeff VanVonderen. *The Subtle Power of Spiritual Abuse*. Bethany House, 1991.

Kinnaman, David and Gabe Lyons. *unChristian: What A New Generation Really Thinks about Christianity...and Why It Matters*. Ada, MI: Baker Books, 2014.

Kouzes, James M. and Barry Z. Posner. *Credibility: How Leaders Gain and Lose It, Why People Demand It*. San Francisco, CA: Josey-Bass, 1993.

Lambert, Frank. *Pedlar in Divinity: George Whitefield and the Transatlantic Revivals*. Princeton, NJ: Princeton University Press, 1994.

Lotz, Anne Graham. *Wounded by God's People: Discovering How God's Love Heals Our Hearts*. Grand Rapids, MI: Zondervan, 2013. Kindle edition.

Mansfield, Stephen. *Healing Your Church Hurt: What to Do When You Still Love God but Have Been Wounded by His People*. Carol Stream, IL: Tyndale House, 2010. Kindle edition.

McIntosh, Gary L. *There's Hope for Your Church: First Steps to Restoring Health and Growth*. Grand Rapids, MI: Baker Books Publishers, 2012.

McIntosh, Gary L. and Samuel D. Rima. *Overcoming the Dark Side of Leadership*. Grand Rapids, MI: Baker Publishing Group, 2007.

Murray, Iain. *Jonathan Edwards: A New Biography*. Carlisle, PA: Banner of Truth, 1989.

Narramore, Bruce. *No Condemnation*. Grand Rapids, MI: Zondervan Publishing House, 1984.

Norton, Howard and Flavil Yeakley, Jr. *Why They Left: Listening to Those Who Left the Church of Christ*. Nashville, TN: Gospel Advocate Company, 2014.

Rainer, Thom S. and Sam S. Rainer, III. *Essential Church? Reclaiming a Generation of Dropouts*. Nashville, TN: B & H Publishers, 2008.

Roberts, Kyle. "Why Every Pastor Should Spend an Hour on ExChristian.Net." *Patheos*, August 17, 2015. http://www.patheos.com/blogs/unsystematictheology/2015/08/why-every-pastor-should-spend-an-hour-on-ex-christian-net/

Ross, A. P. "Psalms." *The Bible Knowledge Commentary: An Exposition of the Scriptures: Old Testament*, edited by John F. Walvoord and Roy B. Zuck. Wheaton, IL: Victor Books, 1985.

Smith, Chuck. *The Word for Today Bible: New King James Version*. Costa Mesa, CA: Thomas Nelson, 2012.

Stafford, Tim. "The Church's Walking Wounded." *Christianity Today*, March 1, 2003. http://www.christianitytoday.com/ct/2003/march/9.64html

Stoop, David. *Forgiving the Unforgiveable*. Grand Rapids: Revell Publishing, 2003.

Toussaint, Loren L., Owen, Amy D., and Alyssa Cheadle. "Forgive to Live: Forgiveness, Health and Longevity." *Journal of Behavioral Medicine* 35 (June 2010): 375–86.

VanVonderen, Jeff. *When God's People Let You Down: How to Rise Above the Hurts That Often Occur Within the Church*. Minneapolis, MN: Bethany House Publishers, 1995.

9 781595 559579